MW00603716

GLIMPSES of the WARRIOR WITHIN:

My Journey of Discovering I AM ENOUGH!

ISBN- 978-0-578-75817-6

LOC#: 2020907438

Publisher and Editor
Mother Daughter Publishing
Atlanta, GA.

GLIMPSES OF THE
WARRIOR WITHIN
My Journey of
Discovering I AM
ENOUGH!

by
Diedra Y. Cole

TABLE OF CONTENTS

The Foreword

I am delighted to write this foreword, not only because Diedra Cole has been a friend and colleague for many years, but because I also believe deeply in the omnipresent laws that govern our universe; the laws that are definite proof that we become what we think about. I also believe that teachers at every level and stage of their career can enrich and strengthen their teaching by learning the principles of empowerment through resistance, patterns and practices presented in this book. Diedra shares her story with courage and pride, and clearly in the presence of pain and transparency.

Over a long and fruitful career, Diedra Cole has explored the philosophy and practice of a warrior within. She has conceptualized the intellectual foundations of introspection, elaborated its distinctive pedagogy, studied its patterns and impact on her life, family, friends and students. Not only do I endorse this book as an author myself but as a reminder that we all have a warrior within, a spirit that is synonymous with each breath of life, each thought of survival, and each moment earned in the awakening of prioritizing and embracing the love of self.

Diedra Cole takes us inside her thinking as she reflects on her achievements as a daughter, mother, leader, teacher and incredible woman. In following her extensive examples and close-up analysis on life, we get a grounded understanding of each phase of her life's experiences. It is humbling to realize that even a skilled and masterful leader like Diedra Cole considers sharing her deepest thoughts and memories, chooses to do so, and advances the right move, and complete this work of art. It is inspiring to see her make the decision to be greater and to awaken the warrior within ourselves and to aspire our highest objectives.

Diedra Cole has produced this powerful tool for serious and sustained personal development, focused on a core practice that belongs in the repertoire of all women, leaders and teachers. This book can help you develop a shared vision and understanding of personal power and its flexible uses in everything you do.

Reading this book, you will find it hard to defend the view that good people are born, not made. Diedra Cole provides compelling evidence that a core lifestyle practice like taking charge of your life and discovering your calling, can be taught and learned, but not without serious and sustained effort. What better way to strengthen the quality of loving yourself first? Reading this book will become a supporter for all who interprets its soul-meaning to thrive, and the riches and privileges of the ability to choose.

Dr. Farid Zarif
ND, PHD, MPH
Beverly Hills, CA

The Introduction

As long as I can remember, my life has been a constant journey of fighting and defending. As a competitive martial artist, I fought to win tournaments. As a middle child, I fought for validation. As an African American adult, I fought being discriminated against. As a police officer, I fought to keep peace. As an advocate for equality, I fought for justice. And as a woman, I continue to fight for respect. Since it is clear that God did not create or design me to fit into anyone else's mode, it is no mystery that my strong spirit power has well kept me from being a follower; what I always have been though, is a fighter.

Despite childhood trauma that trailed me into adulthood, I have always fought to find and live out my God given purpose to help and inspire others. Being a lifelong Martial Artist and having the prestige honor of making history by being inducted into the 2019 Ancient Alpha Warrior Martial Arts Hall of Fame, I decided to title this book GLIMPSES of the WARRIOR WITHIN: My Journey of Discovering I AM Enough! With more than four decades of disciplined training, learning, fighting and self-defending, Martial Arts has been a gift that has blessed me with some of the most gratifying and rewarding experiences.

Ironically, in my everyday living, I found myself using some of the very same defense mechanisms that I spent years mastering in the arts such as blocking, covering up, hiding, etc. as survival tactics for life, too. Outside of Martial Arts and even within (thanks to Sensei Pedophile), my formative years were surrounded by hurt, rejection, isolation, molestation, substance abuse and a very painful silence through all of it. Through every unorthodox, out of the box and challenging hand that I was ever dealt, and even those that I chose, it has been my faith, my consistent training and my continued diligence to press toward my purpose that have kept me afloat and helped me to withstand the pressures of life. I decided not to be a victim but to be victorious by turning my journey into valuable life lessons of hope through courage, wisdom, strength and growth.

I grew up void of knowing and understanding the true power and meaning of self-love, self-respect, self-worth, self-validation and self-care. Without the comprehension and knowledge of your own value and significance, there is always a greater risk of seeking acceptance and approval far outside of yourself.

Furthermore, there is high probability that if left unaddressed, this lack of awareness will have one searching for love in all the wrong people, places and things, ultimately settling for far less than what you deserve, as I often did in the past. It was not until years later when I had an epiphany of discovery that "I AM ENOUGH" and had been so all along! It was at that pivotal point when I made a conscious choice to finally begin to embrace my warrior within. As you read this book throughout its entirety, my goal is for you to embrace yours too. Find peace with your past so that moving forward, you will have the joy and clarity of vision that you need to create your best life and live it to the fullest...void of regret!

~ Diedra

9

CHAPTER 1

Adapt and Adjust, Young Warrior!

Both of my parents were born in the South, my daddy in Alabama and my mama in Mississippi. They were equally hard-working, and both instilled the core value and ethics of hard work into us early in life. My daddy insisted on making me get my first summer job when I was just ten years old. I started out as a Commandos neighborhood street sweeper initially, but within a week I was promoted to riding in the company truck and responsible for passing out bag lunches through the window to the other kids (including my own brothers) as they continued to sweep the streets. Because they were my family, I always made sure they got two! My mother was our caregiver and also a full time nurse and my father was an Army Veteran, full time skilled laborer, worked part time as an aide in the public high school system and was even an entrepreneur and owner of a tavern called "Hard Times" and no he was not Jamaican! In his younger years he was an all-around star athlete and semi-professional football player.

Some studies suggest that middle children struggle the hardest to find their place of belonging. In my personal experience, more often then not, I felt somewhere stuck in the middle, consistently having to adapt and adjust. I was born child number three from my mother's womb and the sixth born of my father's seed. Both my parents already had daughters around the same age when they met, and they bonded as sisters. They were seven and eight years older than me. Soon after, my parents began having children together and eventually my brothers and I came along. I was born in the middle of the two of them. When I was a teenager, (after eavesdropping in on my father's telephone conversation) I learned that I had three additional older brothers living in Illinois that I had yet to meet.

I was raised in Milwaukee in a two-parent home. I was the youngest girl and for the first two years and eight days of my life - I was the baby. After that my baby brother came along and from the three children that my parents had together, I was undoubtedly the "middle child." Mama said that initially I was not too excited about giving up my role as being the baby and that I would defiantly take his bottles and even tried sitting on him one day while they had him lying on the couch. Of course I do not remember any of that.

I am glad that I didn't hurt him because this same baby would grow up and become my protector and defender more than a few times in my life. I do however remember that my baby brother was very sickly throughout his childhood, suffering with chronic asthma. Having to spend (often times) extended stays in and out of the hospital, naturally my mother had to provide extra needed care for him. There was another time that she told me of when I was around the same age of two, that while playing outside on the concrete steps of our first home on 23rd and Garfield, that I fell and hit my head on the steps, knocking myself unconscious. Mama said our neighbor, Mr. Brown who lived across the street from us, took her and I to the hospital but by the time we arrived, I was already up, ok and playing again.

There would be a few more times during my early childhood days when I would fall and hit my head, usually while running and playing outside. In every occasion, I would need to be taken to the emergency room with a concussion. Thankfully, after each time that my brain was bruised, whether from falling on my own or if someone intentionally caused me to fall, like for instance the time when a mischievous neighbor, upset because I had beaten him in a race (being fully aware of the fact that when I ran, I did so with my head held high), purposely placed an object in my path and plotted for me to fall and I did.

Nevertheless, by the grace of God and the warrior within, I was able to overcome.

Isaiah 54:17 No weapon formed against me shall prosper.

I have a glimpse of my mother walking me to school when I was just five years old. It was a big day for me, my first day of kindergarten! We walked hand in hand from my maternal grandparent's home which was only about a block away from my new school. It was during fall season in Wisconsin and I was completely captivated by all of the colorful leaves on the ground along our short walk. I enjoyed my elementary years at E.L. Philipp School and also developed some close friendships. I stayed in the same public school (which was in a black mostly middle - class neighborhood) until the fifth grade. After that, as part of a newly state mandated integration program, I was one of a few students from my school that was unexpectedly chosen to participate. As a result, this meant that I was being forced to leave my school, my friends and my familiar environment. They were busing me to a predominantly all white school with no friends in a completely strange and unfamiliar neighborhood that I never even knew existed. I was not thrilled about it, but I made my best attempts to adjust and adapt. My new school was nothing at all like my old one. I did not have any friends in the beginning, but God sent me an angel in the form of my teacher, and she helped me adjust to what was a complete culture shock!

On the home front, naturally I was somewhat of a tomboy and tried at times to fit in with my two brothers who were close in age. They really did not care to be bothered with me most of the time and we often fought and argued more than we got along. Many times during those fights, they would push me into a dark closet in the living room of our childhood home and use their bodies to press against the door so that I could not get out. I kicked, fought and screamed bloody murder until they would finally back off or until someone else would intervene. Looking back in retrospect, this could have been the onset of some claustrophobic issues that I once lived and suffered with for years. As kids we said and did stupid things to irritate each other. One of the crueler things they often said to me was that I was adopted and that our parents found me in the garbage can. This would make me fighting mad every time they said it. Although we were only kids, it still upset me.

I "over-stand" now (what I did not before) just how powerful our words are. According to Proverbs 18:21, "death and life are in the power of the tongue, and they that love it shall eat the fruit thereof". Regardless of intent, once we put them out in the atmosphere, our words automatically attach to them the power to do one of two things...whether in the spirit or in the natural, our words simply bless, or they curse.

My mother was not very big on a lot of hugging or showing open and public displays of affection. That was just her. In retrospect, I do not recall being lovingly or even casually told "I Love You" by either of my parents growing up. I heard it from my father occasionally but that usually was midstream one of those old school butt whippings that he freely gave out when he would say, "I love you more than I love myself". In those instances, however, it was tough for the love part of his message to resonate. All I could think about precisely was the extreme pain I felt from the stinging of my behind (both during and after) the hits from his leather belt. In retrospect though, I do believe that the whipping's and tough love helped keep my brothers and I in line and out of trouble. There is a debated biblical proverb (Prov.13:24) of sparing the rod and spoiling the child that his choice of discipline could have been driven by. What I do know firsthand is that my daddy had me scared straight and I feared his wrath!

A sweet, soft spoken, kind and compassionate soul by nature describes the innermost parts of my mother. Although she has rarely been emotional or openly expressive to me about her feelings, my mother has always shown me "love in action" in her own way throughout my journey, which has been anything but a straight path. An even keeled and steady temperament like her Libra zodiac suggests, is what I observed her display most of the time. Remaining calm, balanced, even-tempered, sane and mentally healthy could not have been an easy feat for her after giving birth to all but one Gemini child and being married to a firecracker like my Virgo daddy for so long, yet she managed to. I admire my mother's strength, character and her resilience. I am thankful for each of the life principles and lessons that were taught to me by my parents as they lived them by example. They instilled a hard work ethic and many other values in me. Ultimately, they taught me what they knew. I will forever honor my parents with the utmost love, gratitude and respect. One of the greatest gifts given to me aside from the gift of life was being introduced to the Martial Arts world by my father the day he took the initiative and signed me up for the YMCA Karate classes.

The Recap:

Growing up, things like knowing the value of self-love and the importance of discovering God's purpose and plan for my life were not mentioned in my day to day environment. Even though they were not discussed or pushed at home, perhaps they were at other times. I vividly recall my grandparents, the late Reverend Sidney Conner and Mother Lula Mae Conner picking me up on Sunday mornings and taking me to church with them. I would ride in the front seat of my grandfather's Ford, ironically in the middle of the two of them.

Once at church, I would sit in the front with my grandmother on the Mother's board where she served. I'm sure my COGIC grandparents were praying and laying hands on me. Ultimately, God still used my father to assist in assigning me and my purpose to one another. He also used the gracefulness, dignity and beauty of my mother to give the best example of what a Virtuous Woman is.

Although a lot of adapting and adjusting would be constant for me both early on and throughout the course of my life, all roads along my journey were (and still are) leading me exactly to where I am purposed to be and therefore I am Grateful.

Chapter 2

Somewhere Stuck in the Middle

In this chapter, I refer to my position in my family as being somewhere stuck in the middle.

Even before I was introduced to martial arts, in retrospect, I had somewhat of a defensive nature as a middle child. It usually cautioned to protect me against the typical horseplay and sibling rivalry that came along with childhood but the need to isolate also followed me into adulthood. For a long time, I felt somewhat of a disconnect between myself and some of my family members. Growing up my brothers had each other that they could relate to and my older sisters had each other to do the same. However, yours truly was void of a solid sibling connection. In spite of our family being pretty close knit in our own way, the lack of a core connection often left me feeling overlooked and misunderstood.

However, since I was unable to comprehend or understand the isolation that I felt, being able to clearly and fully express or verbalize it seemed impossible. As I unsuccessfully tried for years to process and make sense of this bizarre dynamic, it was not until I was finally able to let go and remove myself from the hurt and emotions that were attached, that I was able to see things clearer and accept them for what they were. Since this was such an unnatural thing for me to have to contend with in the first place, it's no surprise that finding peace with this was undoubtedly one of the most difficult journeys I have had to endure but thanks to the warrior within me, I did. Here's a glimpse of what that looked like from my perspective: Coming together traditionally and occasionally for different holidays, celebrations and events was the norm and I was all for it! During those times, partaking in good food, laughter and an occasional glass of wine here and there was great!

Moments like these actually allowed me to feel more connected to my family. No judgment intended, there were also times when some would prefer to indulge and engage in other levels of mind and or mood-altering activities that I did not partake in, whether by personal choice or by conviction. Although no one in my family tried to sway me into doing anything that I did not want to do, the fact that I didn't engage still brought on further feelings of isolation, separation and disconnection. Especially after it eventually crossed over to involve someone that I brought into the family. Signals were missed and lines were crossed repeatedly.

It was easy to get caught up, consumed with and confused by so many different feelings and emotions running all over the place. Over a period of time and relative to being triggered by certain things and events that transpired, the isolation, separation and contention that I experienced within my family grew deeper. On the surface, things appeared one way, yet in reality they were quite different.

For years I gave my time, energy and efforts into showing up and being present in many ways and in various instances for those who I loved and considered family. The only thing(s) I innately expected and wanted in return was for the same loyalty, sentiment and concern to be shown in action (not words) back toward me, particularly during the times when I was in need the most. After all, isn't that what a "Family" naturally does anyway? At least that's what I thought. However, at the end of the day to sum things up, many times what I got back instead was selectively being left out or uninvited to things, along with an ongoing lack of support, a lack of empathy, a lack of understanding and yes, an absence of loyalty. Although initially I didn't (and still don't completely know to the depths of what degree) this only further revealed to me why I felt so under-valued in some of those relationships. It was draining for me both mentally and emotionally and left me feeling some kind of way during that time.

In times past, whenever the disconnect feeling would surface, I tried to ignore it because it felt so unnatural and uncomfortable to digest. For quite some time, I learned to live around it, but it was always a challenge. I would try to periodically express
my concerns with different family members by attempting to have open dialogue about my feelings, only to be brushed off or dismissed. I would get responses such as "you need to let that go", or "don't start." It became clearer to me over time that no one involved was interested in hearing my perception of things for obvious reasons I guess. However, as time went on and more occurrences ensued, that odd feeling of disconnect eventually manifested itself into something else that (to me) more resembled disrespect and it would all eventually come to a head and have to be faced and dealt with accordingly some how or another.

Word to the wise, no matter what the nature of relationship, it can still be a heart wrenching lesson to automatically expect for someone to respond or show up for you in the exact way that you assume or think that they should. Another mistake often made is to assume that just because someone is blood related, that they are obligated or guaranteed to be there in the same way and manner in which you showed up for them when they called on or needed you. I have met some of the most amazing people farther down my bloodline and even outside of my bloodline completely (perhaps you have too) who have shown me more family support than those that I used to **automatically** expect support from and based on their actions, I consider them not only to be a blessing from God, but also family too.

To be clear, I am not saying nor insinuating that my family was never there for me because "yes" they have been. However, (from my perspective) over time, the build-up of disconnect that later evolved into what I interpreted as multiple accounts of disloyalty and disrespect, in my opinion, went beyond assumed familial bonds and ties. We have all heard at one time or another the famous cliché that blood is thicker than water and personally, I believe that it absolutely should always be. Unfortunately, I can bear witness from experience that sometimes the saying really is just that of a famous cliché. The truth is that in my reality, at times…water has proven to be thicker than blood. Ironically however, I have always felt a special connection and bond to the beautiful children in my family and love being around them. They've always seemed to gravitate to me, and I to them. Many of my nieces and nephews, especially the babies, have always made my time spent with family extra special. I am grateful for that.

All that being said, due to the urgency of my need, goal and desire to heal, thrive, survive and live my best "I AM ENOUGH" (drama free) life in peace, it was imperative for me to find a better way to reposition myself in order to get "Unstuck." Metaphorically and in the natural, the Warrior Within me has been in boot camp preparing, (even from childhood) and adapting to all the vast and fast moving events and changes in my life long before I discovered my God given purpose and full potential or even had a clue as to the true reason behind why I was "different" or called to be set apart. Nevertheless, God has not missed a beat in placing the right people in my life and along my path at the right times throughout my journey. He knew who I would need and who needed me, whether for a reason, season or a lifetime and I'm good with that.

When God has chosen you for greatness, it is likely that your path won't always be a smooth sailing one. Do not be alarmed or get discouraged if you find yourself "standing out" like a sore thumb more than you fit in. I know it's easier said than done but trust and believe that your uniqueness was on purpose and not a mistake, so embrace that!

Although I never envisioned or wanted to go through life with feelings of isolation or separation from any of my own family, I know none of it caught God by surprise. So since He allowed it, there surely has to be some good lessons and even hidden blessings in all of it.

Romans 8:28 KJV~

And we know that all things work together for good to them that love God, to them who are the called according to His purpose

The Recap:

For years, I felt somewhere stuck in the middle and unable to vibe or deeply connect on a regular with some members of my family, all of whom I love. This saddened me internally. However, I am aware that none of us (including myself) are perfect and that we are all indeed a work in progress, striving to do and be better. Personally, I am now focusing my energy on doing the internal work required to improve MYSELF. This includes taking long looks of self reflection in the mirror to help me recognize and work on fixing my own faults and shortcomings. One big one being to learn how to ask for and accept help when I am in need. I have always sucked at that. Self improvement is a daily goal. My heart is open to forgiveness and bridging gaps. Overall, I am thankful that my family and I still manage to be pretty close knit.

It gives my heart much joy to acknowledge that we are in a better place today and are taking strides and making more effort to verbalize and show our love for one another. I am very happy about our level of growth and my sincere prayer is for God to bring more love, healing, understanding, joy and especially PEACE for each of us individually and collectively.

Chapter 3

Dojo Values

The discovery and development of my love for the Martial Arts

By the age of around nine years old, I discovered along with my brothers, a love and knack for watching and then imitating what we saw in the old classic karate flicks. You know the ones where their mouths would be moving as fast as their hands and feet and it was nearly impossible to make out what was being said but the movements were so dynamic that it didn't even matter? Well one day, during this phase, my father came home from a long day's work and told us that his co-worker was studying Karate. Perhaps with the intention of preventing us from either injuring ourselves or each other, he asked us if we wanted to go take some "real" Karate lessons. Of course, we were over the top elated! With as much enthusiasm and excitement that you can imagine, our collective answer was "yes daddy yes" followed up by "can we go tomorrow?"

The next day, he took us to the Northside YMCA on 12th Street, located about fifteen minutes from where we grew up in the inner city of Milwaukee, Wisconsin. It was there where I was officially (and somewhat reluctantly at the same time) introduced to the Kempo-Goju School of Karate and would later discover a tremendous love and passion for studying Martial Arts. I say reluctantly at first because reflecting back on that very first day of class and seeing all the other students in their element and doing their thing, I still had yet to observe any of them doing the movements that resembled the fancy jumping, spinning and flying guillotine, acrobatic acts that I saw being depicted on the big screen many times before, usually by Asian actors marketed and depicted as "real karate" or kung-fu!

Nevertheless, I decided to give it a shot since I was there and had begged to go plus Daddy was making sure of it!

After a few weeks of classes, my instructor asked how we liked it so far, my response went something like this: "It's ok but when are we going to learn how to do those spinning kicks and flips and all the other stuff that they do in the movies, the real karate?" He chuckled and then told me that before I could even think about doing that, I needed to first learn the "basics" because it was going to be the basics that would save my butt in the streets, not what I saw in the movies. Needless to say, my age and maturity level at the time did not comprehend "any" of that what he was saying, so I asked my father if I could quit! Because my father had been an athlete all of his younger life, he did not condone quitting and I could tell he was disappointed with me even asking.

I managed to stop going for a short period but ironically one day while trying to figure out the latest skateboard trend, my brothers and I ended up about eight blocks away from our house, across a busy street that we were not supposed to be on and we discovered that the same Karate school had moved from the YMCA and now into an official DOJO! Hence the first African American Karate School in the entire state of Wisconsin had gotten its own home. I could not wait to get back home to ask my father if I could go back. He said "yes, but this time, you're not quitting!!!" I said "ok" and have been going strong ever since. I have kept my word and that was well over forty-five years ago. God had a plan and purpose for my life which included blessing me with a love and a gift for Martial Arts.

Even though it had been just a couple months or so, for some reason or another, I came back with a stronger eagerness and desire to learn then before and gradually as time passed, I started to get it. It was "my strong will" plus the repetition of executing the techniques over and over and over again that were critical components for me in learning the basic fundamentals correctly. The words my instructor previously spoke finally started to sink in.

As more years went by, another thing I began to discover is the truth versus all the myths that I and many others have fed into concerning the history of Martial Arts and the true nature of its origin and conception. My journey of discovery and love for this lifestyle continues over four decades later from the time I first stepped into Mr. Warren's YMCA class. I am extremely proud knowing that it was actually my ancestors who were the original creators. Many different Martial styles were first developed by cultures throughout Africa and Egypt. Even Masutatsu (Mas) Oyama, (student of Gichin Funakoshi and Gogen Yamaguchi) Founder of Kyokushin Karate, mentions in his book (Advanced Karate written in 1970) that the earliest documentation on organized combat originated from Egypt in 4000 B.C.

~The Basics~

The first Martial Arts discipline that I studied was founded by Sensei Charles A. Warren in 1970. He served in the US Air Force and fought in Vietnam where he witnessed many of his friends who fought beside him lose their lives. When a bomb that was only a few feet away from him failed to detonate, he knew that God had spared his life for a reason. That moment would change his life, giving him a new perspective where he was determined to pay it forward by choosing to use his gift to make a difference in the lives of others. So he returned to his hometown of Milwaukee, combining the two styles in which he had studied while abroad, hence Kempo-Goju, the very first African American Karate School in the state of Wisconsin was birthed 50 years ago.

During my youth and beyond, it became the norm for me to live a life that consisted of eating, sleeping, drinking and breathing Karate! I trained several days a week which eventually led to the forming of a unique bond between fellow classmates that became my dojo family.

Since our system's founder (and head instructor) came from a military and traditional martial arts background, his teaching method included strict discipline and total respect on the floor. We trained hard and no excuses or horseplay was permitted or allowed. Push-ups were done on the knuckles for boys and on the palms for girls and they were distributed often. What's now known as "girl push-ups" on the knees was unheard of back then. Holding the position of kiba-dachi (or horse stance) with our knees bent and both arms held out for what seemed like eternity was also a common practice used for multiple purposes. This stance helped to improve balance, strengthen the legs and core, develop better yang energy, improve focus and it was also commonly used for disciplining when necessary.

We would begin each class with meditation to help clear and center our minds, bringing our focus in. After meditating, we would go into our first phase of the class which consisted of stretching, exercising and warmups that lasted roughly thirty minutes, give or take. After being properly warmed up we would get into the basic fundamentals that incorporated kicks, punches, blocks and stances progressively adding elbow strikes, knees and other techniques into the arsenal. We did combination drills up and down the floor and on certain days we would go over self-defense attacks, choke holds, wrist locks, throws, rolls, sweeps and sparring. Since repetition and consistency are key in developing a solid foundation and building muscle memory, as I mentioned earlier, we did these techniques over and over and over again. Additionally, after bowing out of class in the same way that we started, we would then position ourselves in a straight line with our white towels in front of us and in unison go up and down the dojo floor on our knees, slowly and repeatedly cleaning the floor until there was absolutely no evidence of dirt or dust left in sight. Coincidentally, the towel was a part of our uniform. Each student was responsible for bringing their own clean towel to every single class. If we were not already in uniform, upon entering the dojo our gi's had to be folded properly and we carried them over our shoulders with pride. The gi also had to be clean and ironed and if not, there was the potential of getting sent home and not being allowed to train. After each class, we would change back into our street clothes and were required before leaving the dojo to make sure that our gi was again folded properly (towels tucked neatly on the inside) and that our belt was also properly tied around the uniform and that it "Never" touched the floor! One of the many fundamental principles that Mr. Warren taught us in our training and development as martial artists was that the only dirt that should ever be on a student's belt should come from their sweat and hard work and not from touching the floor. To this very day, although many don't follow this practice, I still believe, teach and hold on to it. No shoes were ever allowed on the dojo floor as we traditionally trained in bare feet. On my way out the door, I would put on my shoes, once again toss the gi over my shoulders, go home then excitedly repeat it all over again the next time. Ahh yes, the Good Ol' days. These are but a few glimpses of the things that Sensei Warren integrated in our routine training with the intent to instill discipline, responsibility, accountability and other core values into his students. For these reasons, I am grateful to have experienced this era as a child growing up and studying Kempo-Goju Karate.

From the mid 1970's and well into the late 1990's, I frequently traveled with my dojo to compete with the best of the best on the Midwest open Karate tournament circuit. Although Chicago was the most frequented place that we would compete as a group, we also would go to various parts of Wisconsin, Illinois, Indiana, Minnesota and Iowa, earning recognition and respect as fierce competitors and great fighters not to be slept on. We also put on a lot of exciting demos and high energy skits during that same time period. As I continuously trained and advanced in rank, the basic fundamentals were still repeatedly taught and drilled into me. In time, I was able to execute them effectively and efficiently. One of the main reasons for us competing in tournaments was that it gave us students a chance to test our skill level against others who were from different dojos, styles and disciplines. You also learned what you needed to go back home and work on to improve. Ironically, the theatrics that my brothers and I initially were so bewildered by when we were kids watching the Saturday afternoon matinee karate flicks, was no longer as impressive to me. On the other hand, however, seeing folks who looked like me out there fundamentally demonstrating massive talent on every skill level...now that was extraordinary!

It was the summer of 1980 and I had just turned fifteen years old. I was in the beginning stages of testing for my black belt when at the last minute, Mr. Warren made the decision that I would not be allowed to continue because he believed that I still had more maturing or growing up to do. He said that I would need to wait another year and that after I turned sixteen I could come back and take it. At that particular time there was no one my age or younger in the KG system that held the rank of Shodan (first degree black belt) level. I was disappointed and caught a major attitude about it. Time didn't seem to fly as quickly back then as it does today and because this young "grasshopper" lacked patience, a year seemed like eternity. Fast forward to July 25, 1981, one year later and it was show-time baby! On top of my previous years of training, I had now been preparing exclusively for the past 2 years to take this extreme warrior enhanced test. I was excited and nervous at the same time and my stomach was filled with butterflies. In hindsight, what Mr. Warren really did by making me wait was advance me some additional time that I certainly did need to get ready for what was ahead. Although I witnessed another candidate go through it the previous year, it was an entirely different ball game now that I was "the" candidate.

(The Gaashuku)

The KG Gaashuku is a yearly anticipated weekend outing that can best be described as a traditional Japanese inspired training camp. This event is made up of students from various Kempo-Goju dojos and invited guests. Mr. Warren purposed and designed this occasion for everyone to come together and lodge collectively at an isolated outdoor location different from our regular and familiar training environments. It's held in the summer in Wisconsin at a campsite or on farmland or someplace similar and goes from Friday through Sunday. Overall, as a unified group we adapt and adjust to living the life of Warriors in whatever outside element that Mother Nature determines.

Also incorporated during the Gaashuku is an intense both physically and mentally exhaustive training and testing phase not suited for the faint of heart. Particularly, this applies to the Black Belt Testing process. The ultimate goal is not to quit or give up no matter how tough things get, and things definitely got tough! Personally, not only would this experience force me to dig deeper than I had ever dug before, surviving it would also "without a doubt" be key in helping me (metaphorically) to prepare for life. This process was about to challenge my knowledge, technique, skill level, strength, stamina, endurance and whatever else but most of all MY WILL POWER!

Everything that I was made of was going to be tried in the fire like never before. I was about to be put to the greatest test that I had yet to experience in my sixteen years of life and my still evolving "Bushido" would need to be right there with me every step of the way in order for me to finish and still be standing (literally) when it was over. Let it be noted, that prior to me taking the test, "NO" other female in Kempo-Goju history had ever completed or even attempted to go through this Gaashuku Black Belt testing process. I was the FIRST female and also the youngest candidate at the time to do so. YES, it was a really big deal!

During this weekend adventure, we set up our tents on Friday evening for our sleeping quarters, used outhouses for restrooms and figured out that bug spray was absolutely essential for survival. It was a good thing that I was nota girly-girl because that would have presented another challenge in these conditions. Cell phones were not a thing yet either, so I did not have to contend with that distraction (but the bugs though). After my testing was finally over, my favorite part of this entire experience came to be and still is the calming of the campfire and all that it represents.

Saturday morning started off at daybreak and everyone participated. We kicked things off with at least a mile-long uphill group run around the campgrounds. I would have to do another individual mile run soon, as a prerequisite for my test and that would be timed. After the initial run, we started our group training session, which consisted of everyone collectively going over a variety of things from exercises, basic fundamentals, combination drills, self-defense techniques, etc. We trained non-stop throughout the morning. Finally, around noon, we took a short break and I drank some water to hydrate and attempted to have a piece of fruit or a granola bar. I didn't   have an appetite because as much as I wanted to get it done and over with, my official black belt test had not even started yet! Yikes...this was definitely going to be the longest day I ever had!

My Shodan Black Belt Test

After the break, per tradition and protocol, those who were already black belts made up the panel and assisted Mr. Warren with the testing process. Some of them had previously gone through the same rigorous test and were now happily "on the other side" which is where I was aiming to get to hopefully after this day. They would all get to vote and collectively decide at the end whether or not I passed. In the meantime, I was already exhausted from the day's events but still had to get myself together for a test that was just about to begin... talk about being under pressure. The under-belt testing started off first and the students were separated by rank and were tested on the requirements for their next level. While they were testing, I was taken off to do my mile-long timed run. After that, I was timed in push-ups, sit-ups, and other physical calisthenics. Then on to kicks, punches, blocks, stances, etc.

At one point I was required to hold the position of kiba-dachi (horse stance) with both arms extended out as they drilled me with intensity on my knowledge and history of the system. While I was being drilled quasi-military style (I'll leave it at that), my arms felt like they each weighed a thousand pounds and my legs felt as if they were going to fall right from underneath me at any given moment but they didn't and I endured. As I held on and advanced to the next phase of the test; I had to demonstrate multiple self-defense techniques, multiple attacks, breaking boards, etc.

(still being drilled with intensity by the other side) By now everyone else is already finished with their training and testing for the day and all are seated in the grass and gathered around in a circle like fashion, waiting to observe the main event...starring ME!

The most anticipated and FINAL stage of my test was the fighting. I had to spar (fight) with at least fifteen others, all men, all black belts and all much bigger and physically stronger than me. I had no energy left at this point but was required and expected to still continue on AND to go two-minute rounds with each one individually. Even though by now I was pretty much out of it and internally questioning myself as to why I was even doing it. But I carried on and fought anyway, pretty much having ONLY my will left (aka) the "Warrior Within" which would not allow me to quit. To add to that, I was also encouraged by the men, women and children in the crowd and watching from the side-lines and even by some of the other black belts as they yelled things like "Keep going Diedra, You're Almost There, Don't Quit, etc." To sum it up, I held my own throughout the test and even though I got a good beat down that day, (an initiation some might say) I can guarantee you, "I DID NOT QUIT!" I was informed by Mr. Warren on the following day that I had passed my test and officially had become a Shodan black belt on July 26, 1981. Hence, I made it to the other side! But in all reality this was just the beginning of my Martial Arts training.

The Continuation of My Training Journey

My Shodan test was nearly 40 years ago. I am so blessed and grateful to still be on my training journey today. I will always continue to give homage and pay respect to my home base that is Mr. Warren, my instructor and Founder of Kempo-Goju Karate. He has been a father figure and instrumental in my life since childhood and our bond is unbreakable.

Life in itself is stagnate without evolution, change and growth. I am currently a 6th degree black belt student of Sijo Steve Muhammad (Sanders), Co-Founder of the Black Karate Federation (BKF) and Founder of Ken WingTai Ba, a Science of Mathematical Fighting comprised of Kenpo, Wing Chun, Tai Chi and Boxing. His contributions have paved the way for many other African Americans and other Martial practitioners throughout the world.

In 2019, as part of his 50th BKF Anniversary Celebration, Steve Muhammad held his first Tournament (Karate of the Gods) in Atlanta, Georgia. I was chosen and honored to be the Official Arbitrator for this Historic event. Also during the same weekend at his 80th Birthday Gala, he inducted over Sixty Ancient Alpha Warriors into his BKF Hall of Fame. I was honored to be in attendance and included in that number as an Inductee. Mr. Warren was also present for this event and was nominated and inducted into the Ancient Alpha Warrior Hall of Fame with me. He was instrumental in making sure that the set up and flow of the tournament was indeed a history making success.

In addition, I have incorporated into my training arsenal Streetology Jutsu, with Grand Master Malik Shabazz, Creator and Founder. Fellow Ancient Alpha Warrior Hall of Fame Inductee, Grand Master Malik Shabazz has over 52 years of experience and is well renown and well respected in his craft of expertise. His philosophy of Streetology is seen as a holistic approach to life, extending far beyond the confines of the training hall or dojo. I am excited about what's ahead in my training journey as I continue to aggressively seek to increase my knowledge,

wisdom and understanding as a life-long Martial
Science Warrior, practitioner and instructor.

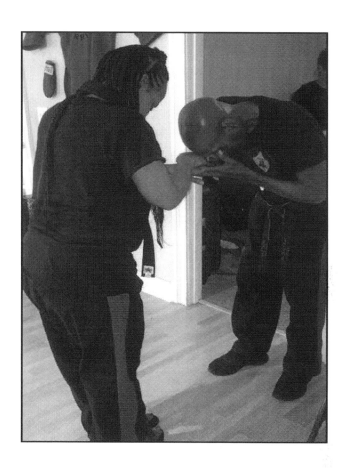

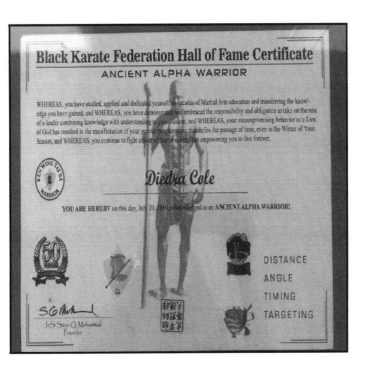

Black Karate Federation Hall of Fame Certificate

ANCIENT ALPHA WARRIOR

WHEREAS, you have studied, applied and dedicated yourself to decades of Martial Arts education and transferring the knowledge you have gained, and WHEREAS, you have demonstrated and embraced the responsibility and obligation to take on the role of a leader combining knowledge with understanding to gain wisdom, and WHEREAS, your uncompromising behavior as a Lion of God has resulted in the manifestation of your genetic programming that defies the passage of time, even in the Winter of Your Season, and WHEREAS, you continue to fight absent of fear or doubt, thus empowering you to live forever,

Diedra Cole

YOU ARE HEREBY on this day, July 20, 2019, acknowledged as an ANCIENT ALPHA WARRIOR!

SGMh
JoS Steve Q. Mohammad
Founder

DISTANCE

ANGLE

TIMING

TARGETING

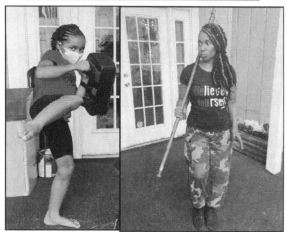

Chapter 4

The Basement Pt. 1
~She Once Was Lost and Nobody Looked for Her~

My room was right off the kitchen and just across from that of my parents. My brothers had their bedroom set up in a corner area of the basement, so they did not see or hear as much as I did. I was however close enough that I saw and heard a lot more than a kid should have to. Often times it would occur in the middle of the night when my father would come home intoxicated. Alcoholics have different kinds of personalities when under the influence and my daddy's personality would sometimes escalate into the "angry" kind. During those times, his tone was scary and abrasive, and his demeanor was that seemingly of a mad man. I would be scared and on edge when I heard his car pulling up in the driveway, not knowing what state he would be in. His behavior was traumatizing to me. I was in total fear for my mother's safety and her well-being and I felt helpless because I was just a kid.

I can only imagine the fear and anxiety that she must have lived with firsthand during those times when daddy would cut up. I loved my father but in those instances, I did not like him much at all and could not figure out why she stayed. Although I do not and will not ever condone this type of domestic behavior (no matter who it is coming from), I have to acknowledge the fact that there was still a lot more living, learning and growing up the road yet for me to do. Simply a child, I was not qualified in any form or fashion, to judge her choice. My limited understanding and comprehension of all that was happening was not something meant for a child to decipher. Nonetheless, my spirit still knew that his conduct and behavior was wrong and that she did not deserve it. Later in my journey of life, as fate would have it, a time would come when a familiar spirit would show up and I'd have my own choices and decisions to make.

As a child and teenager, there were many times that when I was angry, upset or hurting, I would retreat to the basement of our childhood home. Now there was nothing warm, fancy or inviting at all about this space. In fact, however, it was quite the opposite and instead cold, unfinished and cemented. It did, however, contain a few crawl spaces in particular that were just large enough in size for me to go inside and sit while hiding out and sometimes even pretending as though I had run away. I would be in the basement for hours in hopes that somebody, anybody, would notice and at least come look for me but it never happened. In retrospect that was a loud cry for some positive attention that I obviously felt that I needed but was not getting. The even sadder part was that no one even noticed I was missing and never bothered to look for me.

For each basement moment that I experienced back then, either literally or figuratively, I became more and more guarded and perhaps in attempts to protect myself, even emotionally detached to certain things. Since I was unable to freely express myself, I kept my feelings encaged and bottled up inside while my mind traveled to far away places. Those unresolved basement "trips" followed me. How could they not have? I have always naturally been inclined to help or serve others in some way or another. For a long period of time, however, the idea of someone being willing or desirous to help or assist me in the same way (without it being an underlying hidden agenda), was just another far-away thought. Nevertheless, I learned some important life lessons during part one of my basement journey. I realized that even though it felt like it, I was never alone. Although my flesh nature was not yet in personal relationship with my God source (or my creative source) it is clear to me now that spiritually, even as a little girl, I have always been connected.

When my mind was incapable of deciphering a lot of the things that were happening to and around me, I am convinced beyond a shadow of a doubt that angels were dispatched regularly to aid, guide and assist me. God has always been with me, within me, walking beside me and holding my hand. I had to go inside and battle my own demons and fight a spiritual warfare concerning my soul. Too many hindrances, and unimaginable life interruptions to give more than a glimpse, but by God's grace and mercy, ultimately I withstood them all. One of the most arduous things was having to lose some folks along my journey.

TD Jakes says it best, the gift of GOOD-BYE is sometimes necessary. I too have been blessed with that gift and operating in it when needed has been my saving grace.

Discovering the value of my own worth is something that I personally had to fight hard for and dig deep inside to find. Although it required me having to go into some dark and uncertain places (i.e. the basement), it was all necessary.

The Recap:

For each of us, "doing the work" is something that has to be done individually and intentionally and with a made-up mind. Since I made the choice to do my work, (which make no mistake about it, is an ongoing process) I am now validated to share a glimpse of my personal journey in hopes that it reaches others who may struggle with feeling isolated, alone or unworthy. If you are having or had a basement experience, know that you are not alone. May you be strengthened and empowered as you also seek to find your light. Once you do, (and given the effort you will), let your light shine brightly! In the process, hold on to and refuse to let go of your "Peace" that surpasses all understanding. Believe beyond any shadow of doubt, that You Are Enough!

~Philippians 4:7 (KJV)~

"And the peace of God, which surpasses all understanding, shall keep your hearts and minds through Christ Jesus."

Chapter 5

Dojo Violations

My Trophies + My Scars

Winning all of those beautiful trophies and accolades was a phenomenal feeling and this whole karate tournament cycle had developed into a crazed obsession that I lived for! Participating in tournaments regularly included a fair share of unsupervised or improperly supervised over the road travel. This in turn exposed my beautiful, young, gifted, naïve self to a lot. As a result, I endured heavy hardships that my immaturity and youthful mindset had not yet developed the capacity to process or handle appropriately and neither should it have had to so early on. Nevertheless, I placed bandages over each scar (i.e. wound) and internalized it all instead of seeking help and healing properly.

When I was an innocent young girl, I was inappropriately touched by an adult who I trusted. This violation, manipulation and crime occurred while he was being entrusted by parents to operate in a position of guardianship, leadership and authority in their absence. My offender was a Karate teacher who I looked up to and for all intents and purposes, will fittingly refer to him here simply as "Sensei Pedophile".

Note: Parents, make sure that you keep your kids close. Create a nonjudgmental environment for them in a safe atmosphere where trust and an open line of communication is well-defined. If not, they may end up carrying heavy burdens of unnecessary shame and guilt into their adult life that could have been avoided or managed sooner if they had someone close they could talk to and trust.

I remember it was a cold, Sunday, Midwest evening and I was barely thirteen years old. The team was on the highway and the car was full. We were headed back home to Wisconsin from Indiana after a long tournament day. I was excited and still on cloud nine after just taking first place in my division and winning another beautiful trophy to add to my growing collection. Of course I felt safe, I was in the back seat next to a trusted teacher whom I looked up to and had been around many times before. Ironically, this was the same person who earlier that day had coached me from the sidelines as I fought and won, match after match cheering me on. "You're doing great Dee, keep up the good work!" Wow, what a self-confidence building experience that day had been for me. It proved all my training and hard work at the dojo was indeed paying off and spoke for itself on that day. Little did I know, it would be a glimpse that was short lived.

With a three hour or so ride ahead of us to get back home and my mind and body in need of rest and recovery from the massive adrenalin rush it had gone through all day, I innocently drifted off to sleep. I covered myself underneath my coat and as I was drifting off, Sensei Pedophile secretly and shamelessly made the choice to put his hand down my pants. Still partially asleep and completely in shock, I sat up and turned to look at him but his slimy a** was shushing for me to be quiet with his other hand. I was so young and naïve, still a virgin and oblivious to what this nearly thirty-year-old man was doing to me.

My emotions shifted quickly from the excited feeling that I just had prior to falling asleep and anxious to get home to show off my trophy, to instead feeling extremely confused, ashamed and depressed about what had just happened. Sensei Pedophile ruined not just that moment for me but countless other moments down the road were ruined as a consequence of what he had done to me.

The sad thing is he eventually went on to start his own dojo. I cannot help but wonder how many other students had to endure similar trauma at the hands of this person's inability to control their sick lustful desire to have sexual contact with minors aka "innocent children" who had at some point trusted and looked up to this person for guidance and protection. Even though the child is supposedly there to learn how to defend themselves, they are essentially still defenseless in terms of age, maturity and skill level against an adult teacher. Mainly and more specifically, one who is a pedophile and decides to use tactics like manipulation, power over and control while preying on children and waiting for the perfect opportunity to take advantage of the child's inability to defend and protect themselves physically, mentally and emotionally not to mention, potentially leaving them with scars for life.

Unfortunately, over a span of time, I learned of more undercover perpetrators in gi's who were either directly or indirectly associated with the dojo environment. They also used their position of "power over" as they lurked and took advantage of different opportunities and occasions where parents would not be around. Tournaments created the perfect set up for these kind to allure impressionable students using various tactics of manipulation. They had the unsupervised space they needed to make their moves or at least to plant their seeds of intent. Just like a manipulator does, they would continue to further water the seeds they planted with their tactics each time they had the chance and opportunity to do so.

This behavior was a total abuse of power and trust that was pretty shocking due to the level of professionalism, skill and respect demonstrated by them as martial artists on the dojo floor. I did not know how to deal with it at the time, nor did I feel like I had anyone that I could open up to and talk about it. I do however remember when rumors about this type of misconduct surfaced after a fellow instructor who was about to branch off and start his own dojo wrote letters to parents making mention of alleged inappropriate behavior going on. My father asked me if anyone had bothered me. I said "no" because I thought that if I would have told him the truth and knowing my father's fiery temperament, not only would he have taken matters into his own hands and possibly took some lives, but for sure it would not have ended well at all for any of them. I was still afraid to say anything after being shushed in the back of the car by Sensei Pedophile.

Another reason why I said nothing was because I did not want to stop training due to the love and obsession that I had for karate. Although my Warrior mindset was already on the inside of me growing, it was nowhere even close to being fully developed yet. By no fault or wrongdoing of my own, I was damaged. Spinning around with little or no direction and focus, letting life happen to me. Lead by fear and a lack of direction, wisdom, knowledge and understanding, I kept all of this heaviness buried and internalized it for years to come.

At nineteen years old, I got involved with an older man who I first met a month shy of my sixteenth birthday. We first met at a karate tournament. He was ten years my senior. A series of major events transpired between us. I had not yet reached the maturity level, nor did I possess the life skills to properly know how to handle any of those things at this young age. One of the major things that occurred included my first heart break. I get tickled when I think back of my father saying to me, "he's got your nose so wide open that he could drive a MACK truck through it!" Daddy was right. Afterwards, I relocated on a whim and a rebound to Atlanta. This was in the mid 1980's.

A few months after my relocation, a childhood crush who I had not seen in a minute and was now attending Clark College reached out. He invited me to join him for a training session at the campus karate club. We met several years before and had kept in touch off and on. Because he was cute and I was trying to get past my heartache, I foolishly overlooked his previous psycho behavior and outbursts. Some time before, he made troubling comments and threats to my ex over the phone and expressed his anger over our relationship. I thought because that all happened a while ago and he had apologized, it was water under the bridge. That was a monumental mistake! As it turned out, this man/boy was still carrying around a bruised ego and a personal vendetta against me and I did not even know it. I was glad about being in a new city with a fresh start and super excited about getting the invitation to go train with the karate club.

After the workout, everything seemed cool. I walked back to Brawley Hall with him to his dorm where I had left my things and within what seemed like just seconds after entering into the room, he literally snapped and physically attacked and assaulted me. I was taken so off guard because in my head I had at least considered him a friend, realizing now that this entire experience had been planned and premeditated. I fought back but this ordeal literally left me in a state of shock! How do you do this to someone that you claim to like? If it were not enough already, now I have this ugly scar to add on top of the previous ones and even more emotional baggage to carry. Suffering with inner turmoil as it relates to all of my experiences with men up to this point was disheveling and I didn't trust anyone enough to talk about it.

My way of coping was through continuing to study and excel in martial arts. It gave me a sense of empowerment and taught me self-discipline. However, being violated and not having a more open and honest dialogue and relationship with family members subdued and distanced me even more. I never really allowed others to get too close after that. Many years later when my own son was about to graduate with honors on that "same" college campus and had lived in that same dorm in which his mother was shamefully violated, I decided to open up and tell my children, whom I consider to be my best friends, about what had happened to me before they were born. It was liberating to a degree to finally open up and get that off my chest. My daughter would also eventually decide to go to the same school, live on the same campus and also excel academically, graduating with honors too. It was as if God specifically purposed to replace the awful memories of the attack which took place years before on those very grounds by blessing me with far sweeter memories to cherish. He gave me beauty for my ashes as referenced in the Bible in the book of Isaiah 61:3 (KJV).

The Recap:

Loving yourself first is vital above anything else. Knowing your self-worth plays a major role in every choice and decision you make. The advice that I would give to my younger self, and to you, is that whatever you are searching for is already in you. Know beyond any doubt that you exist from a place of Royalty and that within itself, makes you magical. It is in your uniqueness that your true beauty lies. Never be ashamed, doubtful or afraid to be YOU! Always protect your energy and if anyone ever violates you in anyway, TELL SOMEBODY!!!

Chapter 6

Refuge Under His
Wings!

~FEATHER DUST~

The year was 1993 and it was a very cold winter day in Milwaukee. After leaving our regularly attended Sunday morning worship service, I was invited out to eat with an acquaintance and her sister. I had not known either of them long, but they seemed pretty cool and we shared a few common interests. After dinner, they invited me over to their place to hang out. Shortly after, it started to snow pretty heavily. As was typical in Wisconsin during that time, and the fact that it was so cold outside, the snow quickly began to stick and accumulate. I was hopeful that by taking them up on their offer, when I did decide to leave, the streets would have been salted and plowed enough so that I could get home safely. My ultimate goal was that my drive home would not be as dreadful. I also knew that I needed to stop and pick up my young son before going home to prepare for an early workday the following morning.

I heard them make mention in previous conversation that they had a pet bird. However, since this was my first time visiting, I had not seen the bird before. Shortly after we got inside the house, one of the sisters went into another room and came out with the most beautiful, colorful parrot that I had seen before on her hand. I watched on as she began to feed the bird food from her own tongue directly into the bird's mouth. I had never seen anyone do something as bizarre as that before with a bird and thought, "wow, now that's strange but ok." When I mentioned it, they informed me that was something they did on a regular basis and apparently by their shared nonchalant attitude and demeanor, they did not think it was a big deal at all.

Nevertheless, time passed on and by now, the weather had gotten very nasty and the roads were really bad outside. They suggested that I stay over and sleep on the couch and I knew if I did, I would have to sacrifice by getting up extra early in the morning in order to still do what I needed to do to make it to work on time. I made a few phone calls to ensure my child was okay and somewhat reluctantly in my spirit, decided to stay. After a while of chatting and catching up a little more, the evening had grown late, and I retired on the couch and off to sleep I went. Well for a while anyway.

I heard (and felt) the continuous sound of flapping and movement very close to me. Unsure of what it was because I was still half asleep, I continued to hear what sounded like it was getting closer to me each time and eventually right above my head and back several times. Finally, I woke up completely only to discover that it was their "uncaged bird" that had been flapping over me all night. I had assumed the bird was being kept in the cage!!! No one told me otherwise. After I expressed what was going on to them, they were (consistent with their earlier behavior), unbothered and nonchalant about the whole thing. I on the other hand, being totally freaked out and having enough of that experience, saw no further point in trying to sleep or stay there any longer, so I left! Fast forward later that same day, (now Monday morning) and while at work, sitting at my desk and out of the blue, I feel a sharp, excruciating pain in my left side. It lasted for about ten to fifteen minutes' tops and then subsided like nothing ever happened. I thought "what in the heck" was that about. Another hour passed and the same thing happened again! The pain was so intense that I literally had tears in my eyes because I had never felt a pain quite like that before. It literally doubled me over in my chair but again lasting only for about ten to fifteen minutes and like magic, poof, the pain was gone! This literally happened throughout my workday about five or six different times. I was concerned and thought about going to the doctor, but it seemed to eventually subside with no aftereffects, so I carried on with my day.

When I got off work, I went to pick up my son from daycare. After being home and settled for about an hour or so, the pain in my side returned and this time it did so with a vengeance. Sharper and more intense than before, the pain refused to let up. I assumed a fetal position on my couch and was completely unable to move beyond that. I could see the terror in my young son's eyes and the fear on his innocent little face. Even though he was scared, he was still astute and sharp enough that he picked up the telephone and called my parents. When they answered he said, "Hello, my mama is sick, and I don't know what to do!!!" My father was home cleaning his chitterlings. They both quickly dropped what they were doing, as my well-being became the immediate priority. He and my mother drove right over to check on me. I lived approximately twenty minutes away from them in an upper level two family house. Once they arrived, my father picked me up and put me over his shoulders, carried me down the steep flight of stairs and put me in the car. My son was right by my side saying, "Mama you're going to be ok!"

We ended up in the ER at Saint Mary's Hospital, which is the same hospital where I was born. The emergency room doctor, (who was referred to by the staff as Dr. Ni-Ni) was a middle eastern gentleman. After my parents and I explained what was going on, the doctor was as clueless as we were and had no answers as to why this had occurred in the first place and furthermore why it was still happening.

I was in the ER for several hours and still in immense pain with no relief seemingly in sight. Even though the doctor was clearly and admittedly confused, on top of the fact that I was still bent over from pain as I sat in the hospital wheelchair, he initially decided to discharge me and send me home. As he wrote out the discharge instructions, he suggested that I drink some cranberry juice when I got home because I was probably just having symptoms of a bad kidney infection. Fortunately, my folks were not buying into that nonsense. They reminded Dr. Ni Ni that I could not even stand up to walk. After my mother (who was a nurse) firmly insisted that they keep me at the hospital and "not" send me home, the doctor changed his mind and said he would admit me overnight for observations.

During the night, I developed a fever of 105 degrees and as my unknown condition grew progressively worse, I felt nauseous and was very weak. I was continuously given Tylenol as they tried to bring and keep my fever down and under control. With still no explanation or diagnosis of what was going on and a fever that would not break, a specialist was eventually brought in about forty-eight hours later to access me. He immediately ordered blood work and x-rays. The high temperature caused me to be in and out of consciousness, but I remember seeing my mama's face whenever I would be awake long enough to be vaguely coherent. The specialists informed us that the test results confirmed that I had pneumonia.

As I laid in the hospital bed weak and sick already, my mind was boggled from the news of the pneumonia diagnosis since. I was perfectly healthy just a few days ago. The specialist proceeded to ask a question that would forever change the dynamics of this unfolding madness.

"Have you been around any birds?" Due to my state of mind, which was close to delirious, it took me a minute to decipher what was being asked. Although it was only a few nights before, initially I did not recall the incident at the sister's house with their uncaged bird flapping over my head as I tried to sleep over, but then I remembered and nodded my head yes. I was around a bird just hours before I started getting those dreadful pains in my side. The specialists explained that the bird was very sick and that I had contracted bird pneumonia (aka psittacosis or parrot fever) from the bacteria the bird was carrying! He told me to inform the owners. I could not help but think about how freely those girls were with their behavior and dealings with the bird. As I mentioned already, they were even accustomed to feeding the bird off of their own tongues directly into the mouth of the bird. How could the bird be that sick, yet they were both fine? Here I am in the hospital fighting for my life with a fever that will not break and in pain that was unsurmountable.

The specialist brought an article that he printed out to help explain the diagnosis. As it turns out, Psittacosis (or parrot fever) happens to be a rare and very uncommon infectious disease that is most often transmitted to humans through exposure to infected birds, especially parrots, cockatiels, parakeets and similar pet birds. According to the Centers for Disease Control and Prevention, the United States has seen fewer than ten human cases of parrot fever each year since 2010. Usually found in tropical environments (even though we were living in Wisconsin) the symptoms can vary greatly so much so from no symptoms at all (asymptomatic) to severe. It can affect the lungs (which is what happened in my case) and cause inflammatory illness of the lungs, hence, pneumonia and be accompanied by severe muscle pain. The high fever and intense pain in my side was a result of this bacterial infection I picked up from the sister's bird as it continuously flew over my head, flapping around the whole night. Apparently, as the uncaged sick bird freely flew all around the space that I was temporarily occupying, dropping its feather dust, it was also affecting and infecting my lungs.

My parents were worried that they were going to lose me and called on the Elders of the church to pray. One in particular, Elder Yarborough, who has an unselfish heart after God, showed up every day. He would anoint my head with his blessed oil and have whoever was in my room visiting at the time, hold hands around my bed and pray.

The doctor said he would not release me until the fever was gone on its own (without the help of Tylenol). After about the sixth day, the fever finally let up. I believe the Elder prayed the fever away when literally nothing else was working. The owners of the bird also visited me in the hospital. They seemed remorseful but I will never understand how I got sick from their sick bird and they did not. I never even handled the bird, yet they fed him off their tongues!

Nevertheless, I am not sure what ever became of them or their bird or if they followed the doctor's instructions and had it put away. Hopefully it did not make anyone else gravely ill as it did me.

The Recap:

To suddenly get struck with such a bizarre illness, transmitted by someone's infected pet bird, is beyond rare. Furthermore, the United States Census Bureau reported a **population of 259.92** million people in 1993 with only around sixty reported cases. In 2010, this disease is recorded to have infected **fewer than ten people** each year in all the country, that in itself is astonishing! To live through that experience firsthand and be able to reflect upon it now, still blows my mind. I am reassured beyond any doubt that God has always had a plan and a purpose for my life. That bird had something deadly in its feather dust that the enemy tried to use to kill me, but God said not so!!!

"He shall cover me with His feathers,"

Psalms 91:4

Chapter 7

Officer Cole- 53206

~I Think I'll Go Save the World! ~

In my professional career and otherwise, I have always been passionate about helping people. Therefore, it was with great pride and honor that I stood in the presence of God, family and peers and took an oath of office, vowing to protect and serve my community... knowing the ultimate daily sacrifice was the possibility of having to lay down my own life. During my law enforcement years, I worked as a police officer, detective of police and crime scene investigator. Throughout that time, I was assigned to multiple units and divisions. In this chapter, I will share some of my glimpses of this eye-opening journey.

I was already working for a mutual funds company, but the job lacked in its fulfillment of giving me any real satisfaction or sense of purpose on a day to day. Although thankful to be working, there was no passion in what I was doing by a long shot. So one day, kind of randomly and on a whim (or so I thought) I went downtown to city hall during my lunch break and filled out an application to become a police officer. This was the first part of a daunting process that would later involve me having to take and pass a written exam, successfully complete a physical fitness exam that entailed running a mile under a specific time frame, jumping over a six-foot wall (breaking a toe in the process), dragging a heavy dummy, performing a range of multiple calisthenics and ultimately passing an extensive background investigation conducted by the department's Internal Affairs Division (IAD). Oh but the "tom foolery" and unjust actions that followed "after" I had met and exceeded the preliminary prerequisites. I soon realized that this was clearly a warning of the roller coaster ride that I was about to jump myself on to!

Finally, my anxiously awaited letter arrived in the mailbox that would confirm or deny whether I had been accepted as a candidate for police recruit. Based on my exam results, I was pretty excited and felt good about my odds. I also had spoken to several individuals who had already been thoroughly interviewed by detectives from the IAD regarding me and each of them divulged that they believed their interviews had gone well and the detectives seemed quite impressed with my credentials. The short list of people included my pastor, my chief martial arts instructor, past employers and other current law enforcement officers that I had previously been associated with.

Dear Ms. Cole:

"We regret to inform you that at this time you are "not" being considered for the position of Police Officer based on the following reasons: Credit Score, Poor Work History and Driving Record."

The letter concluded by saying that if I did not agree with their decision, I had the opportunity to dispute it by submitting a written letter of appeal which had to be received by them via U.S. mail within 7 days! But here is the kicker: Before I even applied to become an officer, I had recently taken and completed a home buying course and was pre-approved to purchase a home whenever I was ready, so I knew my credit was not a problem. I also received admirable letters of recommendation from previous employers that deemed me as a good employee, so I knew that too was fabricated. Lastly, my driving record was in good standing as it had always been. Something was not adding up and the "warrior within" me was determined to find out. So of course, after initially being pissed off, I wrote and submitted a letter of appeal! A very clear and concise letter I might add that included my letters of recommendation from both former employers and personal references, my home buying course completion certificate, my clean driving record and anything else that I had to refute every lie that had been indicated in their denial letter!

I finally heard back from the Fire and Police Commission letting me know they were in receipt of my appeal response and also when I was scheduled to appear before their board to address my rebuttal. When that day finally rolled around, I was even more eagle eye focused on presenting and defending my case and I felt very confident about my stance on the matter. I reported early to the Fire and Police Commission on the day and time that I was given to pretty much "state my case." What I instantly observed when I arrived was very disheartening. There were several other individuals seated in a very small, dark and bleak hallway, each one waiting for their name to be called. We would each be allotted a fifteen-minute shot to plead our cases before the board as the future of our employment dangled. This actually troubled my spirit beyond measure and to add insult to injury, all of the potential candidates (with the exception of perhaps "one") ironically were African American. In that exact moment, my spirit was even more disturbed. I no longer desired to work for an organization that gave such a bad impression or representation of fairness, nor was I excited any longer over the idea of becoming a police officer. I seriously contemplated turning back around and going home. Instead, something shifted suddenly and my reason for wanting to stay, turned into a silent fury. I saw it as an opportunity for me to walk boldly into the office of the commissioners and calmly and collectively express what was on my mind relative to this whole apparent and blatantly flawed, racist and discriminatory process.

There were three fire and police commission board members present in the meeting - an African American male, a Hispanic female and a Caucasian male. The African American male who was the President of the commission and facilitator of the meeting says to me, "Ms. Cole, boy you really did let us have it in your appeal letter. Now you know Ms. Cole, if you were a police officer you'd have to write a lot of reports. So in those reports while expressing yourself, are you going to let them have it, like you let us have it in your appeal letter?" I said to him, "if I believe that what I'm reporting is the truth then YES I will be writing reports that reflect the truth." The Hispanic lady then chimes in with her piece to say, "well basically, we are just looking for perfect people" (no lie she actually said that to me). I in turn looked her square in the eyes and asked her with all seriousness "please tell me where do you plan on finding those?" She had no comment.

Ironically the Caucasian male said, "well I don't have anything to add or to say in this case. As a matter of fact, Ms. Cole I am confused as to why you are here and why you were not offered the job in the first place because I believe that you'd make a fine police officer Ms. Cole." The meeting concluded with the President informing me that they would be in touch with the outcome of their decision, so in other words, continue to standby. In the meantime, it was disclosed through various outlets that several other African Americans who applied for the position of police officer and resided in the same zip code as I, 53206, had also received the same "exact" letter of denial with the only difference being our names and physical addresses.

A few days later, I received another letter in the mail from them this time congratulating me on the successful "reversal" of their original decision and that they were EXCITED to WELCOME me as a future new police recruit. However, the letter further advised that I would unfortunately have to now wait for the next Academy class to start since I had just missed the start of the current one.

They did not provide me with a date or give a time frame of when this next class would be occurring or how long the wait would be.

So I share this glimpse to shed light on the fact that my fight as an African American Woman in Law Enforcement was met immediately with racism and discrimination coming from different forms of the "in house bureaucracy" of the department well before I was ever even accepted as a Recruit into the Police Academy or before ever responding to my first dispatched call for service while on duty as an official sworn Officer. Now whatever made me think the core of things would change or get better once I actually became a sworn Police Officer and even later after testing and being promoted to Detective of Police, will forever remain a mystery to me.

The truth of the matter is that I have always been a dreamer and believed in the Greater good of humanity. I was raised by my parents to be honest, hard-working and to treat people right. On top of what I was taught, it has been my God given nature to care about the well-being of others. What I was not totally prepared for was how evil and dark some forces and people are and that no matter how good you strive to be or how pure your intentions are, not everyone is made of the same stuff. Values, morals and principles are not magnified, glorified or prioritized in this world and especially not in specific occupations where they absolutely should be. I recall a former seasoned co-worker (who later on down the line also ended up being my squad partner for a while) saying to me shortly after I first started: "Officer Cole, I sure hope that you can swim because just so you know, you have entered into a "Shark Tank." He was not lying!

In spite of the "tom foolery" that continued on and never ceased during my "run" in law enforcement, I can honestly say that the best part of all was being able to aid and assist people who needed help. Some of my most rewarding memories include being selected to work on a few special task forces intended to help families who had lost love ones to sexual assault related cold-case homicides that were yet unresolved. Through the PAL program (Police Athletic League), I was also able to develop and design a martial arts program for inner city children, giving them a chance to learn something valuable that would help to make a positive difference in their lives. My classes highlighted learning basic fundamentals of the arts while instilling in them the importance of self-control, discipline and respect of self and others.

I am a fighter and activist in my own right who spoke out against and protested against racial injustices in the city that I was born, raised and grew up in. I was one of the rare ones who refused to conform and be quiet but instead chose to speak out and even rallied along and marched with my children, my mother and my brother with our community during times of extreme cases of police brutality and thuggish behavior. I bravely did this during my off-duty hours while I was a sworn law enforcement officer, working for the same department being accused. I also suffered backlash behind the stance I took to expose and object against the unlawful activities of racist commanding officers. I watched the very offenders, white males with badges and egos, continue to get promoted and rise through the ranks, while many of my African American peers stood by silently without saying a word. A few chose to commend me privately to say they were proud of the posture I had taken but rest assure, their whispers were no help at all to the cause. There were a few other noble officers who were not afraid to stand along with me, but sadly only a few.

The Recap:

I hope and pray that the day is fast approaching when our people will wake all the way up, drop the self-hate and other self-sabotaging behaviors that only set us back and finally decide to come together. Once we as a people genuinely commit to stand in love and support of one another, then we will surely become the force to be reckoned with that we were originally created to be. In these unprecedented times where the value of black lives still doesn't seem to matter and racism is still running rampant like never before, we absolutely need each other more now than we don't!

(More to follow on this topic in the future)

Chapter 8

Promise Me

~ In the Words of My Daddy ~

Isolated, approval seeker, shame, abandonment issues, harsh self-judgment, over-developed sense of responsibility for others, tendency to confuse love and pity (loving someone you pity), low self-esteem and self-worth issues are just a few symptomatic traits taken from a laundry list created by the support group Adult Children of Alcoholics (ACA)/Dysfunctional Families that I personally found myself able to identify with. The good news is that there is also a flip side to this list.

Tomboy tough on the outside but a wounded little girl on the inside. I am aware now that although much of my described behavior was my endeavoring to "deflect" deep rooted internal scars and secrets, there was also something else going on. Because there was no one I could open up and talk to about things that had happened (and were happening) in my young life, I kept my pain buried deep inside for many years, never telling a soul. Rather than letting it out, I guarded myself and my emotions from the world around me. There was no place that I felt safe enough or comfortable enough to unpack those heavy burdens that I would not wish upon any child. The one place that I did retreat to in order to train, workout and be amongst friends, ironically fostered the opportunity for a pedophilic monster(s) to initiate the onset of some of my darkest childhood moments.

I was born out of my Mother's womb with a special gift. God placed an innate warrior spirit within me via my DNA and from birth, I have had a very strong will. It was already there before my discovery of Karate. If anything, martial arts showed up later in my childhood as manifestation to who I already was, a fighter. I am very clear on this now, but it took some time for me to discover and embrace the fact that there has always been a Warrior Within me with a specific purpose of fighting for me to overcome anything! I grew up in a two-parent household with a loving mother and a hardworking father. Let me be clear, a very toxic and alcoholic hard-working father during my formative years.

There was no real healthy transparency in communicating feelings and emotions in our home at that time. Nobody spoke openly or rationally about their problems or feelings. Lots of yelling, screaming, fussing and cussing from my daddy took place, especially when alcohol was involved.

I remember feeling very nervous and on edge as a child when the monster in him would come out. There were also the times when I feared for the safety of everyone in the house. God forbid those late nights when he would come home and attempt to cook something! He would try to boil eggs on the stove but without fail, he would fall asleep at the kitchen table. The domino effect was that the kitchen was nearly set on fire and consumed with thick smoke, the smoke alarm would in turn go off and wake everybody up, and I would wonder if we should evacuate like we did during the fire drills at school, although this was much more real and scary than that. With my bedroom being close to the kitchen, I could hear all the commotion going on and smell the smoke... sometimes even nearly choking on it. That would be pretty traumatic for anybody.

I cannot remember how many times, after the influence would begin to wear off, daddy would call me to the kitchen while sitting at the table in tears and would say to me without fail, "Diedra Yvette, PROMISE ME that you will NEVER get with a DRUNK, cause a Drunk ain't Shit!!!" He would repeat it with more intensity each time, followed by "Do you hear me?!!" This was back in the late 70's- early 80's era. African American married couples seemed to be more prone then to tolerate and stick it out for the sake of the family or other reasons, no matter how wounded or toxic the person or relationship was. I understand some of the plights and struggles of our Black men a lot better now than I did back then. I can empathize with what they have had to endure while living in this totally unjust world when it comes to people of color. Not to excuse or downplay accountability at all but in hindsight, drinking probably was a vice my dad used to temporarily numb his own pain. I am certain, based on the declaration, that he would consistently make me listen to and promise when I was a child, "don't never get with a drunk, cause a drunk ain't shit", describing what his personal impression of a drunk was while he was drunk, there is no doubt in my heart as to whether or not he wanted to be this way...of course he didn't. Fortunately, as time and life went by, his drinking subsided and the madness that was attached to it faded. However, the long-term consequences from the alcohol abuse would prove to have lasting effects on him and on those around him, myself included.

My father was otherwise a very proud, confident and intelligent man. His wisdom and intellect did not go under-rated and he could hold his own in any setting. Daddy had a natural sense of humor and quick wit that were both bar none. Whether loved or hated, one thing for certain, my pops was not a fake or a phony. Simply stated with him, "what you saw is what you got!" You did not ever have to guess what was on his mind because he had no problem at all telling you and making sure that you knew! He spoke his mind with great confidence and prided himself in the many things he did well and excelled in. He loved family, loved to golf, dressed sharp, had a heck of a hat collection and was a great storyteller with many of his own made up parables, quotes and sayings. My favorite was "use your head for more than a HAT RACK!" which I did not clearly get until much later but totally get now.

He had many friends and when his journey came to an end, his funeral procession was so large that we needed a police motorcade to assist with all the cars and traffic.

Nevertheless, in light of everything, I love and miss him dearly and to some degree still considered myself a daddy's girl. I will forever be grateful to him for introducing me to martial arts. A gift that continues to bless me still all these years later. I am also grateful for the many memorable times and laughs we shared along the way and for all the lessons he taught.

Beyond the flaws (which we all have), I respect him for the man he truly was. He taught me by example to stand up for myself and I'll always have just the right amount of "Dixie" in me to be able to hold my own. My only regret is that I did not get to have him around much longer. I was in my late twenties when he got his wings and daddy was barely sixty. Before he crossed over to the other side, he shared with me that his favorite Bible scripture was Psalms 91. After that, it became my favorite too. I even had it personalized on my license plate.

Before I discovered that I am enough, I never learned what a healthy relationship with a man was or how to choose someone worthy of me. The law of attraction is real. I searched for love, acceptance and especially VALIDATION in all the wrong people, places and things. As a result, what I attracted from my own brokenness was more brokenness. Before my first-hand discovery of the many benefits of counseling, I was terrified of telling my story. I also learned how to detach myself quickly. Maybe this was my own way of surviving and not losing my mind. What I have discovered from my personal experience is that by not seeking or being led to the right kind of help over the years (i.e. counseling or therapy) you only end up adding to and accepting layers on top of layers of dysfunction to yourself and the world around you. The craziest thing is that while in the midst of brokenness, I was still able to be high functioning in several other areas of my life, i.e. school, work, single-parenting of two beautiful souls, faithful church goer, etc., all while going through the motions and trying to be the best person I knew how to be. Realistically in retrospect, it was more like trying to be who the world told me I was. Carrying my pain, scars and wounds, not only was I mastering karate, but I also mastered bandaging and covering up while being emotionally, mentally and spiritually bankrupt!

The Recap:

Below are glimpses of healthy behaviors taken from the ACA list previously mentioned. I too am learning to apply them to my own "I am Enough" life. Please feel free to use and share:

1) Come out of denial about childhood trauma

2) Move out of isolation

3) Stop judging and condemning yourself

4) Discover your true sense of self-worth
5) Choose workable relationships instead of constant upsets
6) Avoid emotional intoxication and regain your ability to feel and express emotions

7) Free yourself from the opinions of others

8) Distinguish love from pity and don't think that

rescuing people that we pity is an act of love

Chapter 9

Around the World and Back Again!

"I'm Going to 'Show You the World,'" are the words that he spoke to me, and he did! We traveled from the Motherland of South Africa to the beautiful island country of Japan, the North Eastern Mediterranean, West Indies and Caribbean, and many more places in between. None of them, however, would compare to the real trip that I was about to go on!!!

Being single most of my adult life and for the last twenty years or so prior to meeting him, it is accurate to say that I was pretty settled in my ways. My status was single and other than once and a while desiring companionship or friendship, I was ok with that. I tried to be in relationships before but had grown tired of the lies and games that people in my region seemed to repeatedly like to play. Therefore, it was my personal choice to take an oath of celibacy. I decided that I would focus on me and when the time was right and God saw fit, the right person for me would show up. Time continued to go by and with the help of my faith and exercising discipline, I intentionally held on to my heart and to myself as best as I could.

We first met at an outdoor festival in the mid 2000's and prior to that day, I had only recently heard of him from a mutual friend and local radio disc jockey who was hired as the show host. Being as though I love outdoor activities and music, when asked if I wanted to accompany him to the event, assuming it would be a great time, I gladly accepted. Actually the host and I dated for a brief period beforehand. When we met, he was still messed up and broken hearted over a previous girlfriend and on top of that he was a struggling single parent dealing with three young children in the absence of their mother who resided in a different state. Being a single parent of two children myself and a busy police detective at the time, it did not take long for the obvious to set in, a significant relationship was not in the cards for our future together. However, what he did possess was a great personality and a pretty cool job that included great music and enjoyable perks (hence this concert).

I vividly remember being inside of the outdoor (VIP) tent eating moments before the show was about to start and the host came and asked if I would take a picture of him with the talent. I walked away from my food and went outside to take the picture. This was prior to cell phone camera days, but I kept multiple kodak disposable drugstore cameras with me, so I was prepared. The host introduced us, I took the picture and in turn he took the camera and captured a picture of myself standing together with the headliner, smiling cheek to cheek. Afterwards, he made the comment "I need me one of those" pointing at me. He probably thought I was a fan but in actuality, I had not even heard of him until a few days before when my friend played one of his songs for me to listen to. His performance was powerful and the music he played was beautiful. The stage presence and energy vibe that he delivered was something I had never witnessed before and on that day I did become a fan.

Fast forward some years later while sitting and chatting with my sister in her living room during a visit to California, I asked if she had ever heard of him. I told her how much I enjoyed the show he put on back home and that I was going to see him perform again someday. She chuckled and told me that he actually performs out on the west coast near her all the time. Well about six years later, my words manifested. I was hired by a local event promoter in my hometown to work as a photographer during an annual lakefront festival in the city. Guess who the headliner was? If that was not enough, I had not seen my radio DJ friend (who first introduced) us in several years either. He had since married and moved away. Ironically, the universe had lined things up so that the three of us were all present once again, in the same place and at the same time. Our mutual friend also seemed to be on a mission to play match maker and hook the two of us up. He asked me if I remembered meeting him and taking the picture and I did. Then he said, "Don't you remember the comment he made about needing one of those, talking about you? He really likes you and just so you know, I've already talked to him and told him that you were here, and he would like for me to bring you backstage to say hi." For a minute I was at a loss for words but then I asked him why he did that. He said, "Well I think you're a great person and I want you to be happy and I want to help get you two together, etc." I mean he was adamant. I was hesitant at first so we went back and forth for a minute and finally he asked me to follow him with my camera saying the rest would take care of itself. He was right. Upfront, he was by all intents and purposes the perfect gentleman. He also was easy on the eyes, smooth talking, chivalrous and extremely charismatic, unlike anyone that I had met before. All of those qualities plus his overall swag struck my interest in a way that was refreshing from the norm.

Usually I am not impressed by much, so it was a pretty big deal. Our friend was determined to make a love connection on that day. He even reached out to both of us after the show to see if he had called me yet. God only knows why he was so adamant, but he was. I got the anticipated phone call and he asked me to meet him so we could talk. I agreed, however, I had my daughter and her friend with me and needed to take them home first. While we were driving, her friend said that she did not feel well and before I could get her home she threw up all over the back seat of my Chrysler 300 (maybe that was a sign) but I was so excited about going back to meet up with him that I was unbothered by the vomit and did not clean it up until the next day because we ended up talking all night!

We continued to stay in touch and a few weeks later he invited me to come out to California to meet him and watch him perform. Without hesitation or a second thought, I said yes! He flew me out to Oakland, and I had a great time. We did some site-seeing near the water beforehand and later I enjoyed the show. After the show, I headed back to my hotel room. We later talked at length engaging in deep conversation that far transcended anything physical occurring. That weekend was the official beginning of a nearly six-year world wind, mind-blowing, head spinning, rollercoaster ride of a relationship. It literally did take me around the world and back again in more ways than one.

Over time, we cruised the Mediterranean, Pacific and the Atlantic Oceans, traveled to Africa, Japan, Italy, Spain, France, Mexico and the list goes on. From the outside looking in, it may have appeared to be a dream life and although there were some wonderful moments, in actuality however, my life during that time was filled with more craziness than I have the time or energy to write about. One thing is for certain, I definitely need to travel back to several of those places again (pretty much all of them) so that I can fully and peacefully partake in all the beauty and great things they have to offer. I missed much of it dealing with pure foolishness.

Truthfully speaking, although I was privy to unlimited amounts of perks that went hand and hand with the lifestyle, (especially being around beautiful live music regularly) most of our travels together, unfortunately, were simply chaotic and dysfunctional. There was an excess of egos, insecurities, alcohol, drama, arguing and many different levels and occasions of disrespect. Peace was not present and I was far out of my element.

Prior to relocating, I found a beautiful home in South Atlanta on the lake. On moving day, our drive from Milwaukee overall was pretty smooth. However, within the first hour of moving into the house, before the car was even unpacked and before the moving truck made it, Mr. Hyde showed up in full effect with absolutely no warning whatsoever! His bizarre behavior, anger and demeanor in that moment gave me a chilling glimpse of the fact that "PEACE" had not moved into that home with us. Even though I tried to ride it out, ultimately I could not deny the fact that if I would have stayed, I would have continued to live without peace. That was too high of a price that I was unwilling to pay any longer.

Here's a glimpse of how those words of wisdom and warning from my daddy all those many years ago, eventually came full circle in my life:

It all started out with so much excitement, vibrancy, intensity and yes, adventure! The connection seemed so divine at first, however, right before my eyes, it seemed to all fall apart. The intensity lingered but the nature of the excitement and vibrancy ultimately shifted and exposed itself into being something else that was vastly different. Whatever that "different" thing was, it was unmistakably on its way to killing every existing part of me, metaphorically speaking. It attempted (and almost succeeded with its fiery darts) to destroy and break my spirit all the while confessing mad LOVE for me. To be honest, the first time it exposed itself was very early on. We had gone on our first real date to a concert in my hometown. After the show, we invited a few family members along to hang. That within itself proved to be a big mistake from the beginning and throughout our entire relationship. Nevertheless, after the consumption of alcohol (and whatever else) he showed another side that was angry and cold towards me. Even though my subconscious felt (very) uneasy like I said in the beginning, I still made a conscious choice to ignore the waving red flags anyway. It is no surprise in the natural sense that I turned a blind eye and a deaf ear to the subtle warning signs that my spirit (gut instincts) was adamant about exposing. I mean after the physical attraction and charismatic charm plus all the smooth talking, world wind romancing, and master manipulation that transpired, it was easy to walk right in and get caught up and caught up I got! The spirit never misguides and there is always a costly price to pay when we decide to listen to another voice instead.

Dr. Jekyll initially presented himself in the most charming and loving way which is not a difficult thing for entertainers to do since performing is their livelihood. Most people are only around them for short periods at a time and only get to see them shining in light of their amazing gift. However, when the euphoria of the crowd and the thousands of fans disappear, Mr. Hyde, eventually has to go home and reveal himself. The act could no longer be contained and after a year or so of togetherness, the flip side of this often misperceived as glamorous or opulent life, started to show up regularly and the naked ugly truth was exposed. These toxic moments were usually driven by everyday substance abuse that undoubtedly assisted in Hyde's transformation process. Paranoia, a mean and angry spirit, ego tripping, false accusations, jealousy and control, a fiery temper, an abrasive and abusive tongue, crazy making and narcissistic behavior followed by unexplained recurring disappearing acts are some of the crops that were produced. On numerous accounts, I was often suddenly awakened from my sleep in the middle of the night and confronted by rage and pathological behavior that reminded me of my childhood.

An old letter written to my therapist years ago prior to a scheduled counseling session while still on my "Trip Around the World" (with the Candy Man):

"After a roller coaster ride on Saturday evening with CM, he couldn't make a decision on what he wanted to do or not do (which is very common with him) relative to sitting in on a set and playing with his friend during friend's show. He was silent during the ride there and when he did decide to use his words, he was short tempered, and slick mouthed towards me and couldn't find anything positive or pleasant to say. We finally make it to the venue and the game/fake face was on!!!! That is, pleasantries toward everyone else but still bitterness and hostility toward me.

He spoke very few words, mostly just evil looks now and again. With his money maker attached to him, he leaves me in the friend's empty dressing room without saying one word! I finally walk out to go look for him and I see him right away backstage where he's skinning and grinning in the face of another woman. I go over and say to him (of course after he's done grinning and smiling with other women as is often the case) "One day you're really gonna regret treating me like SHIT! Maybe not today, but one day." His response was, "What the F--k are you talking about, I didn't do nothing to you!" He pouts off to the dressing room and I go behind him. I told him that he's always walking off leaving me when he's mad, slamming doors, etc. and his response was, among other expletives, "Sit your ass down and shut the F--k Up!"

I looked at him like he was as insane as he portrays at times, then I turned around and left the room. He comes out shortly with his money maker encased and his jacket and said, 'let's go!' As we headed to the car, I asked if he was gonna just leave his friend hanging being as though he already promised to play with him on his last song. He continues on to the car, gets in the car, then out of the car, then back in again. All I could think to myself was, "Whatever! Double minded man!!!!" He replied, "No! I'm not gonna leave my friend hanging but one day you're gonna call my name and I'm not gonna answer." (Side note: Will that be because I've finally come to my senses and gotten the hell outta this craziness I wondered but time would tell)

We go back inside (like bi-polar folks do) and I find a stool backstage and sit my ass down of course while shutting the F--k up! Lol. I watched the show from there. CM goes out on the last song and the Superstar was welcomed with lots of love by the people. It's so good that they don't know or get to see the Evil, Dark and Ugly side of the real man behind the genius talent and good looks. They would be as shocked as I was when I began to see the truth. Sad. After the show while in the dressing room (I'm seated outside with still NO WORDS) he comes out and says, "Dear can you take a picture for me?" I take the pics and we leave. I have nothing to say during the drive to Carrabas for dinner, while having dinner, after dinner or once we made it home.

He had four shots of tequila and a beer. I had a glass of sangria to cope. Once at home, this portrait of a very good man, asks me if I have anything to say to him (well I do but I'm certain he doesn't wanna hear what I really wanna say) so I say no, I have nothing. He tells me that after the cruise (that we're taking Mom on for her 80th BD) we're gonna end it. I say, "cool beans", and walk away to the kitchen. He comes in there and tells me I'm lucky he's taking my ungrateful ass and follows that with "KISS MY ASS!"

I told him that I'll tell him after the fact what I really think of him and he says that he's not gonna listen and for me to "CHOKE" on my words. I told him to remember what he's saying. I also reminded him of the difference in his attitude when he wanted intimacy and that's not how he should speak to or treat a Queen! He stormed out the house without saying where he was going or anything and was gone for nearly a couple hours. I went to bed and tried to go to sleep. Once he got in, few words were said. I did tell him that I've never witnessed him talk to others in the way in which he disrespectfully speaks to me. He didn't reply.

This is how I'm feeling now: (the next day):

Today we've been cordial while seeing one another in passing. I've prepared food and been considerate to him in spite of my deep hurt. It's been a real challenge because truthfully I don't like him right now. My body is sick because of the amount of ongoing stress this relationship has me under. I'm breaking out with rashes on my face and other skin issues. Today I have not been able to stop belching since I got up this morning. It's just not good for my overall health and well-being. I'm feeling very anxious and acid reflux has come back also causing a burning in my throat.

The entire time I was at my sister's trying to enjoy a moment...all I could feel was apprehension and stress.
I became worried if I'd miss a call and worried if he was really upset because I was there (even though he claimed he was not). Worry, worry, worry is all I felt. I did not get the full enjoyment out of my time there. In the wee hours of the night, I'd get negative text messages designed to cause me guilt because I was not in the hotel room with him, that made me feel bad and affected my ability to rest. I did not get one good night's sleep. As a matter of fact, I haven't gotten many of those at all in quite a long time. I keep replaying in my mind my partner telling me last night to kiss

his ass, shut the F--k up and sit my ass down. There's not enough respect shown to me for me to give 100% right now. I'm hurt and vulnerable. The writing is therapeutic, and I feel like that's all I care to do right now.

Old excerpt from my journal:

To turn back the hands of time. Love (or what was referred to as such) should have been better cherished and never disrespected, disregarded and dismissed the way it all too often was. Today's reality is very painful for me and I struggle with this pain. I pray it will soon pass. I do want to move on as well but when I am ready. God only knows when that will be. I need more counseling and therapy because I do not get how so many hurtful things could be done behind the name of love. I need to understand better what that really was and to make sure the part I played in it gets fixed. I do not want to ever travel this road again and repeat any of the ugliness. The emotional, physical and even financial ramifications are far too costly and spread out too widely. Our relationship affected too many other relationships, some which will not ever be the same. Another thing I do not want to do is carry this brokenness over to someone else. I want internal happiness, joy and peace so that I can attract that back to me as a foundation to build on.

The Recap:

While it's certainly ok to be supportive of others whom we are in relationship with...it is NOT ok to get so lost in the shadows, drama and chaos of someone else's life that you lose all sight of your own greatness. There is also "nothing" glamourous or cool about being frequently disrespected, belittled and disregarded. Especially when you know without a doubt that you are worthy of and deserve so much more "RESPECT" than what is being served at the table.

As human beings (especially women), it's natural and easy for us to be led by our emotions. It's our unhealthy emotions, however, that can get us tripped up and cause us to make choices (i.e. do, say and allow things) that bring discord into our lives or into the lives of others. Consequently, at some point, feelings of hurt, anger, shame, guilt, unforgiveness., etc. will surface and will need to be dealt with. We all make mistakes, it's part of life! However, choosing to hold on to past trauma and the negativity associated with it, will literally make you sick! Understand there is extreme POWER in finding your healing and your peace which starts WITHIN by forgiving yourself. We find it easier to forgive everyone else when they offend or mistreat us but we really don't know how to show ourselves that same kind of grace, mercy and compassion. If we don't forgive ourselves, things like anxiety, fear, doubt, low self-esteem, low self-confidence, depression, bitterness, hatred, etc. will be standing close by waiting to take up residency in your Temple.

The good thing is that we are in a day and age where we can reach out and find professional help when necessary. It is essential to our total health and well being "to get and to give" the authentic support and encouragement which we all find ourselves needing at some point. In my personal journey of discovery, I am becoming more self aware and enlightened about the power of forgiveness and especially the power of self-forgiveness. Take your power back...Forgive "YOU" Today!!!

Chapter 10

Take the Leap

As I wrapped up the final remnants of tolerating an unthinkable failing, toxic and narcissistic relationship fused with perpetual disrespect and demeaning character attacks... I had an epiphany! All the time that I had spent crying, praying, and hoping for things to change, it finally dawned on me that things were in fact changing by the minute but not for the better. I was tired of fighting, tired of defending, tired of complaining, my soul had grown plain old tired. Furthermore, on most days other than the person whom I was in relationship with, no one else around me seemed to particularly care that I was overwhelmed, in over her head and on the verge of breaking. I did not say no one noticed because it was no secret that there was a problem but genuinely caring about me was not really in this equation. This made it all the more complicated and confusing. It made no sense to me how the very person who was fueling all the chaos and drama in my life on a regular, was also the same person who in the weirdest sort of way, seemed to cleverly manage to have my back time after time. Hence the dangerous formula known as "crazymaking" disguised as caring, compassion and concern referenced and described clearly in The Verbally Abusive Relationship book written by Patricia Evens.

As my life continued to spiral out of control, I realized that nobody else was coming to save me and that I would have to make some tough and uncomfortable choices that would not be popular in the eyes of the masses; specifically, those who are of the mindset that life should be comprised of and measured by material things, money and status opposed to living a life of peace, harmony and an overall healthy state of mind and being.

I made the mistake of allowing other people who I trusted at the time, far too much access into my personal life and relationship, it back-fired right in my face. This was another tough lesson learned that I want to share. Keep folks out of your business and move in silence, especially when it comes to affairs and matters of the heart. Take your concerns to God first and consider professional counseling. Be prayerful, mindful and very discreet in how much you decide to share and reveal to others because not everyone is your friend.

I was unsuccessful in this area and had to learn the hard way. I discovered during my experience that some family members and a few other people who I mistook as friends were more consumed in self motives and maintaining their own connections due to the status and professional career of the candy-man. I also cannot deny that in a sober mind-set, he often displayed one of the kindest, most giving and generous hearts to myself and to others but the inconsistencies and the maddening behavior was unprecedented. Folks were inaccurate in their perceptions about the great life they assumed I was living and that he was providing. As a matter of fact, some even witnessed the dysfunction and disrespect up close and personal yet at the end of the day other than occasional lip service, their loyalty was not to me. This was a hard pill for me to swallow and I absolutely had my moments behind it. I can say with unwavering conviction if the situation had been reversed regarding any of them, loyalty to my family "first" would have been my choice out the gate! It would not have mattered who their significant other was, what occupation or title they held or how charismatic and charming of a person they were. Family loyalty should outplay all the fluff, or at least in an ideal world like the one I was living in inside my head. I learned that not everyone shares that belief, or at least selectively they did not.

Fortunately for me though, I came to realize the change that I was deep in search and need of already existed on the inside of me. It no longer mattered what other people's opinion of me was. The only way that I could get to it and take heed was to "escape" from the torment of where I was, both literally and figuratively. So after lengthy contemplation, I made the tough choice to leave. Not having any resources saved up or even a plan after the escape, I knew that starting completely over would be difficult and scary, but I could no longer afford to give in to my fears or focus on that. The pages in my life where I allowed fear to govern and rule me had gotten "raggedy" (in the words of my friend's mother) and was no longer an option for me. God's grace is sufficient! He strategically sent me an angel in the form of an extended family member who aided me tremendously by providing the necessary and adequate basement space in her home that I needed for the "Warrior Within" to rise and to live! Saving myself required me to shift my focus and be very intentional about doing the vital internal and external work that only I could do.

Because I know God loves me unconditionally and I am His child, He confirmed several things for me in the process. One major revelation that I got was that despite the level of hurt that I have experienced and endured, family was, is and will continue to always be a blessing one way or another!

Learning how to "let go" and step outside of my comfort zone into a land of unknown, solely led by my faith, belief and desperation for change, has simultaneously been the scariest and the most fulfilling thing that I have set out to conquer. Change is NEVER easy nor is it designed to be. However, what I have learned and can personally attest to is that rather than running away from it, when you instead take a firm stance and decide to face it head on, you will experience a personal growth like no other and discover that you are so much stronger than you could have ever imagined. There are some things in this life that a price tag cannot be placed on; peace of mind and being true to who

God made me are at the top of my list. I will not even pretend that the process of transition and transformation was or has been a cake walk. As a matter of fact, many days it was quite the opposite. However, what I can honestly say is that taking the leap of faith brought about an inner peace that I did not have before. This kind of leap most definitely requires a made-up mind. Yet know that no matter what you may have to give up, there will be some incredible blessings waiting on the other end of the struggle that you absolutely must not allow FEAR to impede upon.

Fear will cause us to hold on to that which no longer serves us, it will prolong the "BETTER" that awaits us and stand boldly in the way of our elevation to our next level of greatness. Fear steals our precious time while forgetting to remind us that the hands of father time cannot be reset to go backwards, only forward. Although God's grace is all sufficient, you still must not allow yourself to be tricked, fooled, deceived or paralyzed by false evidence appearing real. Before I took my leap of faith, there was an internal war going on due to my resistance. Fact is my spirit power had been speaking and revealing undeniable truths to me about the reality of things for quite some time and I was listening. However, although I was listening and even dreaming vividly about what needed to be done, I still refused to take heed because it was not what "I" wanted to hear or do. I prayed, hoped and believed that "LOVE" in itself would be enough to cover the multitude of sin, disrespect, abuse etc. that was occurring and hoped that somehow things would magically fix themselves and get better so that life would be lived happily ever after. However, that was not the case. I chose to ignore the signs and turn a blind eye to all the foolishness that was constant. In essence, the change and transformation that my spirit was crying out for was already birthing on the inside of me waiting for "ME" to free it! Whether good, bad or indifferent, the choices we make do become the life that we live.

The main reason I continued to put up with any of it and for as long as I did was because of my own self-love deficiency. From many years of being unaddressed, it evolved into the unhealthy state that it was in. To bandage and re-bandage something as a means to cover it up does not equate to healing. Until I began the process of dealing with those damaged parts of me from childhood on into my adult life, they were destined to continue to show up. I had to acknowledge them first and then start intentionally loving on myself more. This began an integral part of my on-going healing process. If I knew and understood the magnitude of self-love and self-validation from the beginning, then my definition and expectation of what love from the outside should look like would have been altogether different. Love should never cause you to lose yourself or have to compromise who you are. It should not be jealous, envious, manipulative, abusive, disrespectful etc. or cause you to feel the need to act out in any of those ways.

Subconsciously I knew the day would come when I could no longer hide from my truth: I am enough, and I am the only one responsible for making my own life great. I made a conscious choice to no longer be anyone's victim. I had to let go of past failures, bitterness and blaming and I forgive those who hurt me. At this point it does not matter whether I get an apology or not because it is irrelevant. I have got my own back now and I chose to put all of my energy into unapologetically loving my divine self.

As I invite you to share glimpses of my journey, my sincere hope and desire is that you are inspired to rise above whatever fear it is that you have been allowing to hold you up from reaching your divine purpose. I also hope to help anyone in need who may be facing similar challenges now or down the road. What is it that you know you need to let go of but because of fear, you have not? What you or others may have looked upon as a failure can actually turn out to be the very foundation of your success because You Are Enough!

I found a wonderful therapist who helped me by giving me valuable tools and advice on getting my life on the right track. This process has not been easy by any stretch whatsoever but invaluable in terms of growth and discovering my self-worth.
Protecting my spirit, energy, surroundings and vibrations are now ALWAYS my priority. I am a lot clearer too, about my goals.
I have learned a lot of hard lessons but something the enemy or anyone else has not and will not be able to ever take from me is the fact that I am a true reflection of my ANCESTORS
who were Kings, Queens and Warriors. I too am a Queen, a Strong Soldier with a fighting Warrior Spirit etched within my DNA. I am driven and determined to pay it forward by helping others overcome through battles that I have already endured and by the Grace of God - Conquered!!!

"The relationship was broken by vicious words that slammed into her mind like a sledgehammer. These statements assaulted her consciousness, shaping her as a failure. If he could annihilate her consciousness, he would have more control over her."

Patricia Evans
The Verbally Abusive Relationship

The Recap:

In Becoming the Greatest Version of Self:

Love yourself fiercely!
Accept what happened
Take responsibility

Forgive the past

Forgive yourself
Find your God given purpose and pursue it
Rid yourself from the opinions of others
Do things that make YOU Happy
Repeat!

Tools that are helping me in my journey:

My Faith in God
Prayer and Fasting
Meditation
Studying the Bible
Self-Help Books, Videos, etc.
Speaking Positive Affirmations Daily
Service to Others
Martial Arts Training and Teaching
Protecting my Energy

Chapter 11

The Basement Part 2

~ So I Found Myself! ~

I thank God for family. To be exact, it was my extended family that really showed up for me when I was in dyer need of help but too proud and did not know how to ask for it. It was my extended family and even others who were non-blood relatives that became the family I needed when I needed family the most. Because I had not fully learned my lesson about the importance of self-validation in showing up for myself, there still were those times when I expected others to show up for me and when they did not I ended up feeling hurt and disappointed. However, the lesson I did learn is that when you least expect it, pain can actually be a catalyst to a blessing in disguise. Nevertheless, it all worked together in pushing me closer to my God given purpose.

Seemingly I had lost my way. I needed support and God knew just who, what and when to send. Nothing else can compare to having a true "Support System" in place. There were several angels sent but particularly my beautiful cousin Robelyn who during a very trying and uncertain time in my life, God assigned her as my earth angel. Not only did she offer me a place to stay while I was unemployed and struggling but she also drafted a detailed plan of escape several months prior to my leaving the toxic relationship that I was in. She did this without ever trying to convince me or talk me into leaving my situation. Instead, her words to me were "cousin" only you will know when you've had enough." She went on to say, "I nor anyone else can decide that for you."

My cousin shared with me during our conversation about a recent event where a former employee of hers failed to show up for work one day. It was unusual because this employee had an established account of being hard working and reliable. It was rather out of the ordinary for her to miss work especially without even a phone call. Later that evening, while at home and watching the local evening news, the headlining story was about a domestic related murder suicide where the husband had killed his wife and then took his own life. She was shocked (to say the least) to discover that the victim was indeed her same employee that hadn't shown up for work earlier that day. Expressing to me how very disturbing this was to her spirit partly because she was completely unaware that the young lady was secretly living such a troubled life. My cousin also wondered if there might have been something (anything at all) that she could have possibly done to help her had she been made aware. "I HAVE TO SAVE MY COUSIN" (speaking of me) are the words that followed next out of her mouth.

Although the relationship that I was in was particularly far more verbally, emotionally and mentally abusive than it was physically, still...ANY form of abuse is unhealthy, unsafe and TOXIC! Make no mistakes about it, things have a propensity to escalate very quickly and at any given moment they can go from bad to worse. Factoring on top of that, when someone is participating in manipulation and control and different unknown forms of substance abuse are a constant (with ego and fame playing a starring role), anything is possible. As it turns out, from my perspective and tolerance level, this relationship was brewing daily into a horrifying, combustible mess and we were the perfect recipe for an explosion waiting to happen. The lid was about to blow off at any given moment. My spirit was well aware long before I that the way in which we were dealing with each other needed to end and sadly if it remained the same, it would be the death of me. My spirit was also well aware of the fact that there was more much living still left inside of me. The spiritual warfare was REAL! I endured too many sleepless nights to count and

I cried a river of tears along the way, yet little did the enemy know the fight was already "fixed" in my FAVOR and the Warrior Within me was never designed to quit but purposed to LIVE!

Deciding on when I would jump ship from this off and on, up and down, hot and cold, crazy-making, rollercoaster of a ride was a hard choice that needed to be made. The most difficult part about it was that I did not hate him but actually quite the opposite. If I could have willed things to work and be different I certainly would have. God knows I tried that theory for a long time but to no avail. Like my cousin said, only "I" would know when the time was right, and it was MY choice and my choice alone to make.

I had started praying specifically quite some time before for God to give me the strength to leave. We tried counseling and that experience only confirmed the obvious for both of us. Oil and water was not going to ever flow smoothly enough to become consistent in its flow. I suppose it was not meant to be forever for us in the sense of being together as a couple but sometimes (depending on the situation) we can want what we want so bad that we continue to ignore major signs and warnings until after a while the crazy can appear to be normal or bearable.

The attempts to want to end things in the past were usually followed by apologies and grand gestures. For example, like dropping down on one knee in the jewelry store with the most beautiful diamond ring in hand that my eyes had ever seen and proposing to me while on a cruise ship in the middle of a beautiful ocean on the other side of the world in front of fans and my mama... after being a monster to me the night before. Whew, the extreme measures that were taken and the limits that were pushed are unbelievable and difficult to describe. I was an emotional mess! After the toll this had taken on me, it was hard for me to trust my own judgment. I did, however, continue to pray for strength, peace, clarity and direction from God, knowing full well that he had not forgotten about me. Several months after the escape plan, I did it, I took the leap and left. I abandoned the beautiful home which sat on a beautiful lake but was furnished inside with all sorts of ugly, negative energies and demonic forces from the beginning (even after having the saints come in to pray). I moved into my cousin's basement that she casually referred to as being unoccupied space. In that basement I found an abundance of peace and solace. Once I finally got far enough away from all the foolishness, I wondered what had taken me so long!

As time passed and healing took place, I can look back and see what a great teacher this person was for me in my overall growth and development. I did not see it before because I was so clouded by my feelings plus all the drama. It was in my basement experience (literally and figuratively) that lasted about a year when I began to focus on my healing. I knew that there was an "Amazing Queen" trapped inside dying to break free. I've spent most of my life giving away my power and my time to everyone else.

I allowed others to hold my pen in their hand to attempt to write my story. But since no one can tell my story better than me, I am taking back my power and my pen! As a result, in my transformation process I am not only learning to do things differently but also to think differently. I started to study more about protecting my space and energy and also re-visited the magnitude of operating in the law of attraction. I also have learned the vast difference between religion and relationship with my Creator and I will live the rest of my life on my terms and will do so unapologetically.

The Recap:

The "Basement Part 2" was a divinely ordered step by God to redirect my focus and make my crooked path straight so that I could go and find myself, finally. I have been putting in the work, so that moving forward, I only attract to my life the good things that I know and believe in my heart I deserve and that are deserving of me. An abundance of love, favor, divine health, divine wealth, purpose, wholesome quality relationships, goodness, joy, happiness, creativity, longevity and peace is my portion. If that is also what you want and desire in your life, do the work and make whatever adjustments you know that you need to make.

~Find or Make a Way~
There is "ALWAYS" another way!

Chapter 12

My Warrior Heritage in a Glimpse

I have always been curious about my African heritage, the history of my ancestors and wanting to know where and who I came from. I knew that the history books given to me to read and study in school as a child, did not depict my truth. I felt it in my gut and that is probably why U.S. History was always my least favorite subject in school. I barely passed those classes, however, when finally, I was able to take classes in African American History and Studies, I aced those with ease every time. The "Truth" was purposely missing in those other classes and my spirit knew it!

Personally for me the importance of knowing and understanding my heritage and where I come from is simply that it provides a needed sense of pride in knowing the truth verses all the lies previously told and taught about us. The late Carter G. Woodson, an African American historian, created Negro History week in 1926 to ensure that school children be exposed to black history. His hope was to build upon the already rising popularity and interest in African American culture represented by the Harlem Renaissance in the 1920's. During that time writers like Langston Hughes and others wrote about the joys and sorrows of blackness. Musicians like Louis Armstrong, Duke Ellington among other greats, captured the new rhythms of the cities created in part by the thousands of southern blacks who migrated to urban cities like Chicago, Detroit, Milwaukee and others.

Artists like Aaron Douglas, Richard Barth and Lois Jones created images that celebrated blackness and provided more positive images of the African American experience.

By celebrating the heroic black figures, be they inventors, entertainers, or soldiers, Woodson hoped to prove our worth, and by proving our worth, he believed equality would soon follow. His other goal was to increase the visibility of "Black Life" and history at a time when few newspapers, books and universities took notice of the black community, except to dwell upon the negative. Ultimately, he believed Negro History week, which became Black History Month in 1976, would be a vehicle for racial transformation forever. With all of the noble efforts and amazing hard work that he and so many others before us have put in for the advancement of our people there is undoubtedly still so much more work that individually and collectively needs to be done. It is our responsibility to learn, teach and share that knowledge with others...ESPECIALLY with our children who will not get it from anywhere else. Why would we want to deprive them when so many of us were deprived from that source of POWER?

The Legacy of Samuel A. Lindsay:

Over 171 years ago on October 24, 1848 in Monroe County Alabama, Samuel A. Lindsay was born to a pure bread African mother and an Irish father who went by the same name. He later moved to Clark County Mississippi and according to the 1860 Census, the younger Samuel A. Lindsay owned twelve slaves and four slave houses in Monroe County, Alabama which he inherited from his father when he was just eleven years old.

In 1879, now a grown man, he met and married a beautiful young woman from the Choctaw Indian tribe named Ellen Virginia Poe, who was born in Mississippi between 1859 and 1861. Her mother, Deborah Poe, also haled from the same Choctaw Indian tribe. Samuel and Ellen were my maternal great grandparents and together they produced 15 children. My beautiful grandmother, Lula Mae Lindsay (Conner), born on June 6, 1901, was their twelfth child and she in turn later birthed my mother and her siblings.

Samuel A. Lindsay was noted to have been a man of excellence and integrity who loved his family. During a time when racism was extremely overt in Mississippi, he was still adamant on making sure that all the children in his area were well educated. He especially felt that way concerning his own children, so much so, that he built the first school for black children to attend in Carmichael, MS (Clarke County) on land that he owned so that they could be educated. He named it the Lindsay School and it went up to the sixth grade.

My grandmother later met and married my grandfather the Reverend Sidney B. Conner (son of Lawrence and Georgia Ann Conner) and together they produced 6 children, my mama was their baby.

The Legacy of Lawrence Conner:

Lawrence Conner was my great grandfather on my mother's paternal side. He is recorded in the U.S. Census as being born of Mulatto race in Alabama in July 1870-71, just a few years after the 13th Amendment to the U.S. Constitution's Abolition of Slavery. He was the son of Titn and Juda Conner, my great great - grandparents who were both born in the state of North Carolina. Lawrence later moved to Clark Mississippi and married my great grandmother Georgia Ann Conner who was born in March between 1870-1876 in the state of Mississippi (Clark County possibly). U.S. Census records further indicate that both of Georgia's parents were also Conner's; Margerit Conner (from North Carolina) and George Conner (from Alabama). Perhaps they were all somehow connected through the Conner slave plantation where everyone had the slave master's last name. My great grandfather, Lawrence Conner was consequently tarred and feathered to death in Mississippi at the hands of the white supremacist group the KKK which was formed in 1865. This was done while his family, (including his son, my grandfather, Sidney Conner) was forced to watch.

This insidious criminal act was key in my grandfather's ultimate decision to leave the south in the 1940's and relocate his family up north where he settled in Milwaukee on a quest for a fresh start that included hopes of a safer and better life in Wisconsin for his family. My grandfather also served, fought in and survived the First World War (aka) World War I (1914-1918). My mother told me once that one of the main reasons why he left the south when he did was because he was fearful for the lives of his three young sons since racism was so prevalent in Mississippi, making it a very dangerous place for young black men. Once settling in Wisconsin, my grandfather hit the ground running and he continued to prosper. In addition to being an ordained COGIC Pastor, he also started the first African American church in Madison, WI and was a Master Barber and entrepreneur. He owned a barbershop in the heart of Milwaukee's Historic and affluent Walnut Street community where many black folks were thriving.

The Legacy of Alex Cole:

Alex Cole was my paternal great grandfather and he was born on June 7th, 1867 and died on September 11, 1966. I was born on his birthday, nearly 100 years later. He was the son of Horace Cole, my great, great grandfather and was born on the Coffee Plantation in Coffee County, Alabama.

Alex Cole fathered well over twenty children. My great grandmother, Hester Cole, his wife appears to be Native Indian (unsure of which tribe). One of their children, Dixie Cole Sr., of Florence, Alabama, was my paternal grandfather, Dixie Cole, Sr. He married my paternal grandmother, Mary Ragland also of Florence, Alabama and they produced my father, Dixie Cole, Jr.

The Legacy of Richard Ragland Sr. and Margrette Ragland (Smith)

Are my paternal Great grandparents. They are the parents of my grandmother Mary B. Ragland and my Great Uncle Richard D. Ragland and their siblings from Florence, Alabama.

The Recap:

Although tainted from the ugliness of antebellum slavery and all
that went with that, my Warrior roots and history still run far, wide
and deep on each side of my family. I know and understand that I
am here because of the bloodshed, sweat, tears, hard work,
resilience and prayers of my ancestors. They are all Warriors in
their own right, and it is on each of their shoulders that I am able
to stand strong and prayerfully have made and will continue to
make them proud. Family will ALWAYS matter most to me.
"It helps us to remember there is no more powerful force than
a people steeped in their history. And there is no higher cause
than honoring our struggle and ancestors by remembering."

~Quote from Lonnie G. Bunch III, 14th Secretary of the Smithsonian
Institution

My Maternal Great Grandfather- Reverend Samuel A. Lindsey

My Maternal Grandfather- The Reverend Sidney B. Conner
U.S. World War I Veteran – Thank you for you Service!

My Maternal Grandmother- Lula Mae Lindsey- Conner

My Beautiful Mother

My Great Uncle Leroy Lindsey

U.S. Army Veteran- Thank you for your service!

My 2nd Cousin- Robert L. Nicholson, Sr. U.S. Army WWII Veteran.
Served as a Buffalo Soldier and POW (Prisoner of War). He was held
captive until the war was over. Thank you for your Service!

My Grandmother, Lula Mae Lindsey-Conner and two of her three handsome sons. My Uncle's Rev. Samuel L. Conner and Quillie B. Conner

My Paternal Great Grandfather- Alex Cole

My Paternal Great Grandmother- Hester Cole

My Daddy

My Paternal Great Grandmother Margrette (Smith) Ragland

My Paternal Great Uncle Richard (R.D.) Ragland
U.S. Army Veteran- Thank you for your Service!

My Paternal Great Grandmother Margrette (Smith) Ragland

My Paternal Grandparents Dixie Cole, Sr. & Mary B. Ragland

My Lovely and Oh So Beautiful Mama!

My Handsome Daddy!

U.S. Army Veteran- Thank you for your Service!

My Pops (with Family) as a Teenager

My Dad (far right) and his U.S. Army Buddies. Thank you for your Service!

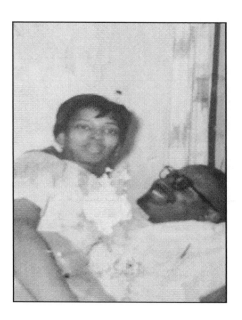

My Beautiful Parents!
Thank you for making me!

Milwaukee's Historic Walnut Street

My Great Uncle Funroe Cole and his wife Aunt Mary Cole

Mommy and Me!

QUEEN~ Diedra Y. Cole (DYC)

Chapter 13

Sisterhood

~A Bond Every Girl Needs~

With life being so unpredictable and times changing right before our eyes, we never know when we may need another sister's support and helping hand. However, the odds are very high that inevitably at some time or another, we will. It is pretty unfortunate that many women (especially those of us of African American decent) are not taught or shown early on the importance and absolute necessity of having a true bond of sisterhood. This reflects in how we treat ourselves, what we accept from others, what we teach and ultimately how we treat our fellow sisters. It is a shame because when we do not have that and are not open to it, we actually cheat ourselves out of being able to live an all-around happier, healthier and more enriched life.

It has been a long and proven fact that we live in a world and a society that does not appreciate or respect the beauty, value and strength of what is "The Phenomenal Black Woman." Instead, so many feel threatened by all of the "WONDERFULNESS" that God placed in our DNA when He created us. Since the Creator of all living things first confirmed how dope we are by making us the "Original Woman" that "ALL" life comes from, I believe it is crucial that we change the way in which we see and treat each other. To my sisters who have not yet gotten the memo, it is time to step up and do better!

It has been my experience that women who are jealous of other women and who make the conscious choice of "hating" on another sister via by using lies, social media and going through whatever other extreme measures intended to attack their character or inflict pain, derives directly from a place of insecurity, threat, fear, hurt or some other internal damage. One thing for sure is that it has far more to do with how that woman feels about herself than how she actually feels about the person(s) she elects to mistreat. Her actions clearly indicate and prove that sadly, she does not even love herself. It was once told to me that simply put, haters are actually your biggest fans who just refuse to admit it. When you do not love yourself, how in the world can you properly love or show love to somebody else? It is imperative for young girls to be cultivated in and around an environment that encourages by example the beauty in embracing and celebrating the special bond of sisterhood.

Women who have the love of God in their hearts and genuinely love themselves don't have the time nor desire to entertain the negative energy required to bring other sisters down. Confident and secure in who they are, real women prefer not to use their energy and resources to tear down another sister with her mouth by gossiping, backbiting, hating, or any other type of ugly conduct. True Queens, solid and assured in who they are, instead will choose to use their time working on bettering themselves while vibrating on an overall higher level of consciousness. Their love and support of one another is genuine and it shows effortlessly in their actions which speak volumes louder than mere words could ever.

Furthermore, their spirit automatically will reject partaking in behavior that reflects anything opposite of a Queen Mind-Set. We want to see each other winning and are excited for and "NOT JEALOUS" of our Sisters.

Sis, this world is big and broad enough for ALL of us to shine! I would never expect or ask of another Queen to give up or dim her light in any capacity just so I can feel better about myself or who I claim to be. Not only is that a ridiculous notion within itself but it is also a clear and sad indicator that "ego" is in charge and is running the show. For anyone who would do or has done that to someone else, please seek help because that low level behavior is indicative of a bigger problem that belongs to you. Even if your outer exterior and image appear to be opposite of your behavior, your actions still speak much louder. Furthermore, your attempts of deflecting how you really feel about YOU on to someone else, are very evident. Whether connected by blood or water, the importance of the bond of sisterhood cannot be overemphasized. It is hard enough being a Black Woman and many of us face the same day - to - day challenges in surviving the world around us.

Since we have been tricked into not knowing and believing who we really are, mainstream media purposely gives a false depiction of us to the world. Social media, the internet and television~ all have aggressively contributed in the spreading and exposing of the hatred, lies and negativity that war against the true Essence of the Black Woman. Unfortunately, we have allowed it. Neither platform shows any shame or remorse in how we are perceived since they consent to our women addressing and referring to one another as bitches and hoes. Sadly, many women even see this superficial behavior as normal nowadays and refer to themselves by those same derogatory names as if it is a term of endearment. Some of the trash Reality TV shows have also heightened this unawareness of who God created us to be. Their images and content feed into the lies and confusion that is already lurking amongst us. The truth is we hail from Royalty and that is a fact! Our Ancestors who carried us on their backs and shoulders already paid the ultimate price. I would not be surprised if they are turning over in their graves in total disbelief.

There is no reason for us to be at odds and in unnecessary competition with one another. The quantity of hate that is exhibited amongst women exceed the crucial need of love and support that can be gained from the bond of "True Sisterhood" and friendship. There is a sad and deep seeded internal hatred of self because we have been conditioned to hate who we are. The famous Malcolm X quote: "The most disrespected person in America is the black woman. The most unprotected person in America is the black woman. The most neglected person in America is the black woman." I will never understand for the life of me, why women choose to do that to each other when we have already been berated by so many for years.

In times past, I too have been targeted by this kind of unfortunate behavior, which in part motivated me to add this chapter topic to my book. The lesson that I personally learned is that in reality, even though we may by nature come from a loving and trusting place in our dealings and interactions with others that compel us to be open to bonding, (especially with those who may share similar interests) however, we must be careful and take heed after spirit has forewarned and shown us when it is not being reciprocated. The Bible mentions in The Song of Solomon 8:6 of jealousy being crueler than the grave. One thing about jealousy is that it brings more harm to the jealous person than to anyone else. It makes you bitter and insatiable with the good things happening around you. God knows the heart of men and He sees the end from the beginning and will deal with things accordingly. Therefore, we must always give careful thought to our actions concerning how we treat others.

Experience has taught me that you do not have to do ANYTHING outside of being your unique, beautiful and wonderfully made authentic self in order for someone to dislike or hate you. They don't need a reason. Like I mentioned earlier... their energy, personal insecurities, ego, attitude and actions, stem directly from how they really feel about themselves. Trust and believe~ this is NOT about you so keep right on shining like the big and bright star that you obviously are. Let your light illuminate without wasting even one second of your precious time or energy playing small or being triggered by DRAMA!

The Recap:

I am at place in my life now where I am blessed to finally be a part of an amazing sisterhood. We laugh out loud together, we cry together, bounce ideas off of each other and help one another to grow. The thing that affords us to be able to authentically do that is the fact that we all genuinely love, respect, honor, cherish and support one another in our different dreams, goals and aspirations.

Negative energy like jealousy, ego and hatred does not and cannot exist or thrive in our environment. Although we are Queens and strong forces to be reckoned with in our own right individually, collectively we understand that we are not in competition with one another so therefore Everyone Wins! If you are not a part of a real sisterhood bond like this (be it by blood or water) you are missing out and I pray that you will someday have the opportunity to know what that is, even if it means that you are the one meant to initiate it. Let's Love on each other while we can because life is precious.

~Love and Light to all my Sisters. ~

In Loving Memory of Alexis
August 2, 1964- April 10, 2020

In Loving Memory of Dana
May 21, 1965- April 1, 2020

Dana, your genuine and radiant beauty, your funny laughter, your warm smile, your positive energy and your tender giving, caring and loving heart will forever be remembered. You will live on in all the lives that you touched. Girl, you left us way too soon but your legacy shall remain through your (our) children and on into eternity. Thank you for being a Sister-Friend to me and a Mother in Love to my daughter. You are greatly loved and deeply missed.

Chapter 14

My Children:
~The Heart of a Single Mother~

While pressing through and contending with issues of life, it was clear that none of those things cared anything at all about my goal and aim to write and finish this book. As a matter of fact, there was one specific time during my "press" that I felt literally "STUCK". Nevertheless, the Warrior Within mentality, fueled with determination and drive, kept pressing on anyway to complete what I was mandated by my Creator to do. I prayed and asked God for help.

The noise of life going on in and around me was too LOUD and I needed clarity and direction. I knew that it was merely the enemy sending constant distractions to get me off track. Remember, nothing short of that should be expected whenever he's attempting to abort greatness of any sort, especially when the end result will be positive and beneficial to the masses. I subtly heard God answer by telling me to shift my focus and write about something that makes me happy. The first thing that came to my mind, without hesitation, was my children. Undoubtedly, they are the two best parts of me. They bring me immense joy and I know with surety that I am blessed to have them in my corner! God must see me as a pretty special and amazing Queen to hand pick "ME" to be their mother. As I share more glimpses of my story, I pray that you or someone you know will be encouraged and uplifted.

Admittedly I made some poor choices previously in past relationships relative to whom I have allowed to occupy my personal space and my precious time. In retrospect, I definitely should have been more diligent about asking and seeking God for guidance first and foremost prior to giving any thought at all about who should get the privilege and prestige honor of fathering my children. The truth of the matter is that this is such a critical decision (or at least it ought to be) but for many reasons, some beyond me and some not, I was in a cloudy, smoked haze of unknowing for a long time. Unknowing how dope and worthy I truly was, I undersold my value for many years. I deserved so much more than what I settled for and so did my children.

Based on not knowing how to properly love and care for myself at the time, unfortunately instead I was controlled by haste decisions, temporary pleasures of the flesh and giving the wrong people too much credit way too soon. All of that combined prohibited me from being able to make wiser sound choices and decisions on who I should and should not connect with. Not planning or looking far enough into the future but instead merely living for the moment, I ended up choosing two dead beat dudes who lacked the moral character and fortitude to successfully father my children. In hindsight, not only did I lack the necessary wisdom, understanding and knowledge but I have to reiterate that sadly enough I just did not love, value, cherish, or appreciate my own greatness enough to wait on the King that we deserved and who deserved us. Clearly, I had not yet discovered my own WORTH!

I spent a lot of years trying in my own way to make up my children this vast injustice that I felt I had done to them. I did not do everything right by any stretch but if works alone could get you in, my goodness! It did not matter to God that His daughter had not fully developed into the Queen that I am today. He still allowed grace and mercy to overrule my poor choices. He still sustained me and allowed me to be able to provide a decent life for them as a single parent. There were some struggles, one specifically early on when I had to go on welfare and seek government assistance for a short period of time. However, I knew right away that it would only be a temporary thing because I was determined not to become slave to a system that was likely designed to further enslave the mindsets of certain classes and groups of people. I refused to use this as a crutch to stay in a seasonal predicament that I was in due to not choosing wisely enough.

Even though my children had absent fathers who sucked and shucked their responsibilities of fatherhood concerning my babies, neither of which ever manned up to provide the financial or emotional support that they needed, God still continuously made a way! I am sure that my poor choices and lack of planning affected them in ways I cannot even imagine, but because the word of God confirms that children are a blessing, God's purpose and plan for their lives is still superseding! Nevertheless, God's divine hand and guidance assisted me in setting the example of having a personal relationship with Him through prayer, fasting, diligence, drive, hard work and determination. Both of my children have developed into intelligent, articulate, creative, etc. souls. I have not one but two HBCU Clark Atlanta University Honor Graduates. I am beyond proud of them and even more grateful.

When I was seven months pregnant with DeMille, (namesake Cecil B. DeMille great filmmaker, producer, director) my firstborn, I was involved in a bad car accident and my head went through the windshield. It was raining heavily that day and the tires were bald on the green thunderbird that I was the front passenger in. Several times on the way to the doctor's appointment that I was initially headed to, I asked the driver to slow down but per usual they blurted out some rude comment, refused my request and continued to drive like the crazed maniac he ultimately proved himself to be. I could see the massive telephone pole ahead as the car began to spin out, taking its aim directly towards it and I knew that it was not going to be a good outcome.

I saw my entire life quickly flash before my eyes. Convinced that I was not ready for my child and I to die, I grabbed the door in attempts to get out before the head on collision. The next thing I remembered was lying on a sidewalk near the curb, seeing blood everywhere. I was in a state of shock as I cried out "my baby, my baby". There was a good Samaritan white woman kneeling down on the ground next to me with a gentle demeanor. She grabbed my hand, telling me not to worry that she was a nurse and that my baby and I were going to be fine. I heard her say to someone else "I believe she's going into shock" as she continued to tell me to try and stay calm, assuring me that help was on the way, she continued holding my hand until the ambulance arrived. Of course the driver of the car (who was also the father of my unborn child) did not receive even one scratch on his body.

I arrived via ambulance to the hospital and the doctor (who was also very kind and had great bed side manners) ran tests to check vitals of the baby. The Doctor advised me that by the Grace of God, my baby was healthy, unharmed and intact inside my womb and that there was no cause for concern as to whether or not I'd be able to continue in carrying full term. Before allowing me to see what my face looked like, he informed me that he would be able to construct plastic surgery on my forehead and that overtime my scar would heal nicely. My official due date was October 31st. I prayed for God to please not allow my baby to be born on that day. I did not want to have him brought into the world on Halloween. A personal choice for me because I don't believe in that holiday or the evil and wickedness associated with it. October 31st came and went, and I was still nine months plus pregnant. After being three more days past due, I went to the neighborhood high school track to walk laps as I regularly did but this time with more intensity and desire to drop my load because now I was tired of being pregnant! After leaving the track, I went to Ingles grocery store to grab a few items. While standing in the checkout line, I looked down on the floor and realized that my water had broken.

After going into delivery and getting prepped and checked for vitals, the doctor informed me that they were only hearing a single heartbeat which was my own and no heartbeat was being detected for the baby. He said they needed to do an emergency C-Section in order to save his life. After the baby was delivered and the surgery was over, I learned that the reason that there was no heartbeat detected initially was because the umbilical cord had gotten wrapped around his throat and had temporarily choked him out. In just a few short months the devil had tried twice now (and failed) to snatch his life away. These episodes were an indicator of the greatness and purpose already placed inside of him and confirms that God in fact knew DeMille by name even before forming him inside of my womb, regardless of who his natural father was.

By the grace of God and the warrior essence within me, I was back on my feet and competing in a karate tournament again after only about six months from the time of the car accident and just a few months after giving birth to my son. At this particular tournament, a gentleman (who was also wearing a gi and a black belt), approached me and asked if he could see my face. He said he wanted to look at my scar. I had no clue who he was initially until after he asked me if I remembered him. He went on to explain that he was the doctor who had performed the plastic surgery on my face after the accident. (How bizarre was that?!) He said I told you that I would take care of you and that the scar would be barely noticeable, he was right.

By the time DeMille was barely a year old he was not only talking but also singing and performing. By the age of two, he was leading songs in the Angel Choir at church and also preaching and performing at his daycare in Milwaukee. His teacher said that every morning throughout the week (after I would drop him off) that he would stack up the milk crates and stand on top of them to give a sermon to the other children who would be sitting on the floor gathered around and captivated by his actions. This compelled his teacher to come and visit the church he was attending and to further get up and share with the congregation how she was led there by the daily sermons that DeMille at only two years old, would bring each morning to the daycare. On Sunday mornings, the choir director would kneel down and hold the microphone for him while he would unashamedly sing songs like "God is a good God, Yes He is" and "I love you Jesus, way down in my heart." Then there were the many times we could be home watching a movie and by the time the movie was over, he effortlessly had remembered, recited and reenacted multiple characters' parts. Family members and friends would be so amazed and amused wanting him to perform something anytime he was around. Birthday parties were definitely anticipated venues for a DeMille performance. By the time he was eight, he was on programs singing solos at different churches and different events in multiple Midwest and southern cities.

Today, he is an incredible creative force to be reckoned with and well able to hold his own next to "any" artist who's already at the very top of their game in the entertainment industry respectively (period). As a matter of fact, he has done so already on many occasions without the world-renowned recognition and exposure. God's favor has been monumental in the magnitude of his gifts and talents. Not only do they include singing but also acting in both theater and film, song writing, play and script writing and also directing. Unwavering with eagle eye focus, he has devoted his life's work into polishing and fine tuning the crafts that God gave him so when the time

My beautiful daughter, Tiara (because I knew she would be a
Princess) came into this world around six years after that. This was
following my close brush with death from contracting the bird
pneumonia. By now I am in my late 20's and still figuring this life thing
out. I was grateful to have a stronger family support during this
pregnancy as my Mother, (along with a girlfriend of mine) were right
there with me in the delivery room the entire time. This was my second
C-section and it was incredibly painful and it felt like somebody was
pulling my insides out. However, once I finally saw her face, the pain
was no longer my focus. She was beautiful then and still just as
beautiful now. I am beyond grateful that God sent His Angels in the
form of Uncle Willie (R.I.H) and TT Lawrence (Godparents) to help us
out unselfishly while I pursued my career in law-enforcement during
her formative years. They extended my child so much pure love and
affection and I won't ever forget it.

A gifted writer and visionary who wrote her very first book when she
was just barely in elementary school entitled "The Lonely Girl with the
Red Fingernail Polish", Tiara excelled through all aspects of school.
Eventually, after an array of strong outside influences to go in a
different direction, Tiara chose to listen to her own spirit power and
accepted an opportunity to attend her brother's Alma Matter and
went on to pursue her undergraduate degree from the prestigious
HBCU Clark Atlanta University where she majored in and earned her
degree in Broadcast Journalism, graduating with honors. Currently,
she writes for the Milwaukee Business Journal and various other
publications. Some of her many other gifts, talents and
accomplishments include being an entrepreneur, published Author,
editor, fashion blogger, fashion designer, web designer and future
Humanitarian. Sugh, (short for Sugar) as I often affectionately like to
call her, is just a bright light to the world! She has always been filled
with an abundance of intelligence, creativity and balance with an
equal drive and strong will to match. These words do not adequately
come close to describing her total awesomeness but instead merely
touch the surface. However, the world will soon see for itself because
Tiara is certainly on her own journey of becoming a Powerful and
Phenomenal Black Woman! I do know however, that I am honored
and Godly proud to be her Mother.

Her spirit is kind and her soul is caring and compassionate.
Make no mistake though...she is no push over by ANY
stretch! As a matter of Fact, Tiara is a Warrior and a
Fighter just like her mother but far more advanced in her
critical thinking skills then I was at her age and even

beyond. I am glad that her decisions are routinely based on information that she personally takes the time to seek out, study, research and carefully examine beforehand. She also is my calming voice of reason and knows me better than most. I cannot imagine life without her as my best friend.

As I previously stated, she has been a Visionary from the start. As I cheerfully root her on and as I watch and share her all of her dreams and visions unfold, it confirms for me with absolute certainty that God's Word does NOT come back empty or void. Children are a Blessing from God no matter the circumstances.

Jeremiah 1:5 (King James Bible) says:

"Before I formed you in the belly I knew thee; and before thou camest forth out of the womb I sanctified thee, and I ordained thee a prophet unto the nations.

(Visit her lifestyle blog at tiaralcole.com)

Words of Inspiration

It was 1976, the first year of Wisconsin's mandated integration of students' program. Diedra Cole was a "pioneer" in this program, forced to leave her familiar neighborhood to embark on a new journey. This may have been her first "Glimpse of the Warrior Within". This was a true warrior step as she navigated through new situations in this unfamiliar environment. I noticed immediately that she was a strong 11-year-old girl, that had a love for learning. Her academic skills were excellent, and her confidence was apparent. She was admired by her peers, but made sure she remained true to herself, by not following the crowd.

Teachers try not to have favorites, but it was hard not to admire this kind, intelligent, beautiful child.

I continue to be proud of her today and am thrilled to have been able to stay in contact with her through the years. I can only hope that I was a small part in instilling the confidence and a can-do attitude which she possesses today. Forty-Five years later, Diedra has shown that she is an empowered, insightful, courageous woman who continues to be beautiful both Inside and out.

Much Love,

Lynn Seidel
Retired Student Teaching Supervisor
University Wisconsin Milwaukee

Words from my Son:

When I think of a warrior, I think of Diedra Yvette Cole; not merely because of her impeccable skills in the field of Martial Arts and not simply because of her tenure as a bad-ass female cop turned detective. No, I think of her because she is quite simply a personified version of the word itself - WARRIOR. I have watched her navigate this often-tough terrain called life. When the waves of despair came crashing overhead, I saw her breathe deeply, regather and continue to swim. You know why? Because that is precisely what warriors do. I know the collection of life stories in this book will bless a world of people. I am so proud to witness her turn her pain into purpose. I am even more proud of the fact that I get to call her mom-

DeMille Cole-Heard

~ Son ~

Words from my Daughter:

I could write an entire book on the moments I got to witness the warrior within. Very clearly I can recall my mom working 12-hour shifts to protect and serve as a police officer in the rugged streets of Milwaukee. She would not get home until the wee hours in the morning. She still woke us up every morning and dropped us off to school. She has been present for every major life event. She has been prayerful during every trial and tribulation, all while managing her own life's ups and downs. Although she raised us alone, she made it look so effortless. We never went without. Watching my mom prevail from a long emotional abusive relationship was a pivotal moment to witness. She left what she had grown accustomed to (money and desired lifestyle) and started completely over. I saw her pick up the pieces and succeed like only a true warrior would do.

Now here we are. My mom's first book to help inspire the next warrior. I hope the words written in this book give you a glimpse of what I've seen my entire life. The warrior within.

Tiara L. Cole
~ Daughter~

The Afterword

I give thanks to my Heavenly Father for giving me the ability to complete this project. To transpose into words and release these glimpses of my journey amidst seemingly one nuance after another, took some real girth and spirit power. Secondly, I give acknowledgement and forgiveness to my past. To the curious, overlooked and often misunderstood little girl who was undoubtedly born a fighter. Looking back in hindsight, each experience was a push to thrust me closer to my God given purpose that includes empowering, uplifting and inspiring others who need it. To every tear I have ever cried, to every heartache and disappointment I have ever had to face, to every decision (both good and bad) and the consequences that accompanied, I thank you. For without you, I never would have realized just how strong I really am... nor would I have discovered that I Am "ENOUGH" and had been so all along.

The Dedication

To my Ancestors, I give thanks beyond measure. To my Mom and Dad, I eternally thank you. I am the perfect combination of you both and that has enabled me to thrive and survive without quitting life. DeMille and Tiara, how ironic that God would choose me (flawed and all) to be called "Mama" by two of the most beautiful, talented, unique and incredibly creative souls that I know. Seeing me at my best and my worst throughout this journey, I thank you both for riding with me and for your love and support along the way. You both did an amazing job on creating my book cover too. To the rest of my family for each part you've played in my growth and development, I thank you.

Dr. Farid Zarif, thank you for believing in me even at a time when I did not know yet how to fully believe in myself. I continue to experience a new level of growth and enlightenment after every conversation with you.

My first Sensei, Mr. Charles Warren and my KG family, I am forever grateful to you for providing me with a strong and solid foundation in the martial arts all the way from childhood into adulthood. You instilled in me the tools and Bushido I needed to be able to take my gift anywhere in the world and represent. To my Sijo and friend, Mr. Steve Muhammad (and also Malik Shabazz) thank you to each of you for the profound impact that you've had during my martial warrior transformative stage. I am very appreciative for the advanced level of training that you've shared with and imparted into me so that I could add to my arsenal. Sijo, your kind, humble spirit, your wisdom and humor... combined with your impeccable skills, knowledge and A-1 level teaching of your mathematical science, compounded with your patience and unwavering belief in my ability to master myself cannot be transferred into words. I am honored and Godly proud to be your student and a BKF Ancient Alpha Warrior!

My Warrior Brother Travis Harper. I thank you for believing in my vision from day one. You freely and unselfishly stepped in offering me help and assistance AND you did so without ever having met me before! This confirmed what I already knew to be true ...there are still some genuinely good people left in this often "cut-throat" world in which we live.

Tina Wilcher-Ragland, your strong faith, beautiful spirit, positive energy and giving heart are unmatched. Your supernatural Warrior strength when faced with extreme adversity has always amazed me. Thank you for staying calm while helping my daughter pin my location which ultimately helped save my life when I had that sudden and severe panic attack while driving by myself on that dark and lonely highway that I was traveling on (both literally and figuratively). I won't ever forget that act of love and kindness.

World Shakers International Church family, pastors Dennis and LaKesha Spears, thanks for your constant love and prayers on behalf of me and my family. Also, many thanks for your ability to remain transparent, approachable and real in a world filled with so many fakes and counterfeits.

Dr. Cheri Sims, well what can I say? Your "Faith" moves mountains! Thank you for always exemplifying in your actions the fact that Faith without works is dead!!!

Finally, to my beautiful sister friends, I am thankful that God is the Master planner and that He already knew just how much I needed you in my life AND exactly when and how to make it a reality. While shining brightly in your own lanes, yet still genuine and secure enough internally to uplift, encourage and mutually show me love and support. Now "THAT" is what real Queens and Sisters do and you know who you are!

"When she transformed into a butterfly, the caterpillars spoke not of her beauty, but of her weirdness. They wanted her to change back into what she always had been.
But she had wings."
~Dean Jackson~

CONNECT WITH THE AUTHOR

Diedra Y. Cole, Founder of DYC Martial Arts, was born in Milwaukee, Wisconsin and she currently resides in Atlanta, Georgia. She is the Proud Mother of DeMille Cole-Heard & Tiara L. Cole.

A Custer High School Graduate with a Bachelors of Arts Degree in Human Services & Criminal Justice, this powerful vessel has even served as a Law Enforcement Professional!

As a BKF Ancient Alpha Warrior Hall of Fame Member and Master Martial Arts Instructor, Cole has spent most of her life learning, developing and training both mind and body in Martial Arts. She first became fascinated by it as a young girl searching to find her place. By the age of nine years old, she was mesmerized with Kung-Fu movies and enjoyed watching them in the theater with her brothers on Saturday afternoons. In the early 1970's, her father, the late Dixie Cole Jr. took the initiative to sign her up for Karate classes at a local YMCA, located in the inner city of her hometown of Milwaukee, Wisconsin.

Master Charles Warren, Founder of the Kempo-Goju School of Karate (the states first African American Dojo) was her Sensei. This was the official start of her training journey that would tap into (the beginning) of the awakening of the Warrior Within.

Fast forward some forty-five plus years later, Diedra is still training, teaching and doing what she loves most which includes enhancing her Martial Science knowledge while inspiring many others along the way as a Coach, Motivational Speaker and Independent Beauty Consultant.

Currently, she is a Sixth-Degree black belt student of the legendary Sijo Steve Muhammad (Sanders), Co-Founder of the Black Karate Federation (aka BKF) and also Founder of the Fighting Science of Ken Win Tai Ba. Cole is the proud owner of DYC Martial Arts and remains dedicated to paying her gift forward. She is especially committed to fulfilling her passion of Empowering Women and Girls to Embrace their Warrior Within. Her own life accomplishments are a direct testament of being a lifelong student of the arts. Be on the lookout for more published writings from Diedra in the near future.

This amazing author has been featured in the following:

Film:
Lila and Eve Burden
Night School
The Hate You Give
What Men Want

Television:
Being Mary Jane
The Resident
Black Lightening
Dynasty
Greenleaf

Bravo TV
Blind Date- Martial Arts Instructor

Training
Nick Conti's Professional Actors Studio DeMille Cole-Heard

Contact Information:
www.dycmartialarts.com

Facebook:
https://www.facebook.com/www.dycmartialarts

Instagram:
@Dycmartialarts

For booking info contact: TIARA COLE
Email: dycmartialartsbookings@gmail.com

Phone: 414-841-9141

Support Women Entrepreneurs 24/7
www.marykay.com/dcole2037

Made in the USA
Columbia, SC
13 November 2020